# KNOW THY

# GAMER

# KNOW THY

# GAMER

## A Parent's Guide to Video Games

# Drew Dixon

**B&H**
PUBLISHING
NASHVILLE, TENNESSEE

Published by B&H Publishing Group
Nashville, Tennessee

Dewey Decimal Classification: 794
Subject Heading: VIDEO GAMES /
PARENTING / SOCIAL MEDIA

Cover design by Matt Lehman. Icons by matsabe/shutterstock
and tulpahn/shutterstock. Author photo by Katie Wylie.

For my own growing gamers:
Evelyn, Gwyneth, and Thatcher—may you work, play,
and live for the glory of God and the good of your neighbors.

# Acknowledgments

This book would not be possible without the love and support of my wife Jennifer whose dedication to thoughtful and intentional parenting constantly inspires me. Additionally, my three children, Evelyn, Gwyneth, and Thatcher, deserve thanks for their patience and unwavering love.

This book would certainly not be possible without my mom and dad, Cathy and Ray Dixon, whose unwavering belief in me has given me the confidence to write and pursue dreams like writing a book.

Special thanks to my brother, Thomas Dixon—thank you for being a good friend—one of the greatest treasures of my life is our renewed friendship.

I am incredibly thankful for the thoughtful editing of Logan Pyron at B&H. Also thank you to Taylor Combs and Michelle Freeman at B&H for their support and for helping this project get off the ground.

I don't think I ever would have attempted to write anything substantive about video games and the Christian faith were it not for my friendship with Richard Clark.

This book would be a lot less interesting and a lot less clear without the edits of my good friends and colleagues at Love Thy

Nerd: Madeline Turnipseed and Joey Thurmond who took the time to read the book and provide feedback.

Additionally, I doubt I would have ever had the chance to write a book about video games or would have had the confidence to do it without the support and encouragement of the cofounders of Love Thy Nerd: Chris Gwaltney, Bubba Stallcup, April-Lyn Caouette, Matt Warmbier, and Kate Kadowaki. Love Thy Nerd is a nonprofit ministry whose work would not be possible without the many people, too numerous to mention, who support us financially. I wish I could list all your names, but if you are in the Fellowship of the Nerd, thank you for your consistent and generous support over the last few years. I thank God for each of you.

I also want to thank the editorial team at Love Thy Nerd in no particular order: Madeline Turnipseed, Jon Campoverde, April-Lyn Caouette, and Joey Thurmond. I should also mention my former editors at Love Thy Nerd: M. Joshua Cauller, C. T. Casberg, and Stephanie Skiles. All our editors, past and present, are amazingly talented, creative, and thoughtful people whose work has inspired and empowered me. M. Joshua and I hosted the Gamechurch podcast together for a time, and our late-night hangouts at video game conventions are something I will always treasure.

I should also thank Ben Trueblood and John Paul Basham—their leadership and support has been invaluable. I have also learned a great deal from my coeditors in Student Publishing at Lifeway: Karen Daniel, Brooke Hill, Morgan Hawk, Kyle Wiltshire, Amanda Mejias, and Jennifer Saio.

And Mikee Bridges took a chance hiring me to work for Gamechurch. Thank you for believing in me and investing in me. A loving church home is necessary for any project like this one, and I am thankful to have found one in Grace Story.

I am also thankful for the pastors and mentors who have invested in me spiritually over the years: Ryan Coatney, Stephen Gambill, Brad Williams, Paul Roberts, and Todd Blackhurst. A special shout-out to Brad Williams for his continued friendship and support of me and my family.

And finally, thank you dear reader for buying this book and making the effort to know and love the gamers God has given you. Your investment in your children will not return void.

# Contents

# Introduction

If you've picked up this book, the chances are that your kids play video games. And if they don't, they want to. Video games are fun, creative, challenging, and even empowering. They can also be really difficult to put down. They can even be addictive. And if you weren't worried enough already, many of the most popular games contain graphic violence and even sex. As a thoughtful parent, you aren't sure what video games you should let your kids play—if any at all. This book is a tool for parents to develop a biblical understanding of the value of video games, and of play itself, so that they might help their children get the most out of them and avoid their greatest pitfalls. This resource will aid parents in sifting through the conflicting claims about video games so that they might help their children not only develop healthy gaming habits but also discover how they might engage video games for the glory of God.

# So Your Kid Is a Gamer?

Tim finally did it—the thing he had dreamed about doing for so long. He grabbed the Nintendo DS (a handheld gaming device) out of his son's hands. Jonah had been sitting in the same spot on the family room couch for four hours playing *Pokémon*. His younger brother and sister begged him to play with them while Jonah either ignored or snapped at them. When Jonah pushed his little sister down after she accidentally bumped into him while playing, Tim sprang into action.

As Tim lifted the DS out of reach, Jonah began pleading, "NO DAD, GIVE IT BACK! PLEASE GIVE IT BACK. I'M GOING TO LOSE EVERYTHING!" But Tim had already made up his mind. He looked at Jonah, jabbed his index finger into his son's chest, and said, "We've had enough of your bad attitude, disrespect, and laziness. I will NOT tolerate it anymore. You are NEVER playing this again!" And he brought Jonah's DS crashing down on the tile floor with all the force he could muster, which for Tim, a former college baseball player, was a lot.

Jonah ran, sobbing, to the DS and picked it up to assess the damage. His father was right; he would never play it again; the screen was completely shattered. Jonah looked at his father, tears streaming down his face, and yelled, "I HATE YOU!" before running to his room and slamming the door.

I didn't make this story up, and I wish it were the only such story I've heard. One parent told me about how they locked their son's Xbox in the freezer (which I thought was odd, but points for creativity, I guess). Another told me how they locked their child's PlayStation in their gun safe, which I would highly discourage; children are remarkably resourceful, and you do not want to entice them to figure out how to get into a gun safe. There is even a video that went viral of a parent gleefully placing all their kids' games, systems, and peripherals out on the front lawn and running them over with a riding lawn mower. That last one is probably fake, and the number of parents that bragged in the comments about the ways they've violently disposed of their children's video games is disturbing, but it's also instructive. The destruction of property is never an appropriate form of punishment; however, these stories are instructive because they illustrate a common source of contention that we can no longer afford to ignore: video games.

A few days after smashing Jonah's DS, Tim decided to take a different tactic. Ashamed of the rage monster he had become in that moment, he decided to throw in the towel. At a loss for what to do, Tim's wife signed off on the idea as well. They replaced the device and said: "If you want to spend all your time playing video games, have at it! No more restrictions—play video games all you want!" They hoped his newfound freedom would reveal that video games aren't nearly as fulfilling as Jonah thought they were, but he didn't get the message. Instead, he played more than ever, and all the behaviors that had been irritating Tim and his wife multiplied. Once again, Tim found himself angry and frustrated. And worst of all, Tim became deeply resentful of his son.

My family and I go to church with Tim. Our kids play together, and we've even had each other's families over for dinner a few times. He knew that I helped lead "that game ministry thing." Tim was deeply ashamed of the damage he'd done not only to his son's DS but to their relationship. Tim loves Jonah and recognized that his resentment was a problem so he called me for help.

Tim told me about the DS incident and about how their new hands-off approach was failing. He then proceeded to ask dozens of questions about video games: Should I let my kids play video games? How long should I let them play? What games are okay for my son? What games should we avoid? Should we let him play online with his friends? What about parental controls? Aren't games bad for kids' brains? Will they stunt his growth or his development? Why does he seem like a zombie after playing? Why doesn't he seem to want to do anything besides play video games? Why is he mean to his brother and sister when he is playing? Are video games making him more aggressive? Is he going to get into fights at school or worse if we let him keep playing? Aren't games basically a waste of time? Are games going to keep him from playing outside or getting exercise? We are a Christian family—aren't a lot of games anti-Christian? When Jonah talks about video games, I don't understand half the words that are coming out of his mouth—what are loot boxes? What does "sus" mean? What are creepers, and why are they bad? What does PvP stand for? PvE? DPS? FPS? RPG? JRPG? MMO? MMORPG?

Like Tim, you've probably had similar questions. You probably don't know the answers. You might be frustrated or angry or feel like you don't know what to do.

While I was a little overwhelmed with this onslaught of questions (which we certainly didn't have time to tackle), I told Tim I was proud of him. Tim was completely caught off guard. How could I be proud of a father who broke his son's possessions in a fit of rage? I definitely wasn't proud of that decision, but I was proud of Tim because, for the first time, he was making a genuine effort to understand his son's most cherished hobby. Understanding our children's interests and hobbies is one of the greatest ways to express love for them. Additionally, Tim came to a crucial realization that every parent must come to at one point or another: he needed help.

I could tell that Tim was worried that his anger and resentment made him a bad father. While I would never condone Tim's actions, I knew he wasn't a bad father. Bad fathers don't try to better understand their children, they rarely admit their failures, and they certainly don't ask for help. Tim was doing all three. And in case you're wondering, you're not a bad parent either. Bad parents don't read books about how to understand and love their children.

Tim didn't know what to make of video games or how to help Jonah navigate them without turning into a zombie or turning into a rage monster himself. Tim was never a gamer. When he was a kid, he spent most of his time riding his bike and playing baseball. The world of video games was not only foreign to him but utterly bewildering. He was at a complete loss as to how to help his son navigate the world of video games. He said, "Drew, I am just not equipped to do this."

When it comes to video games, you are probably at a loss too. Like Tim, you may feel like you're just not equipped to help your child. I will tell you what I told Tim: nothing could be further from the truth. No one is better equipped to help your child navigate the world of video games than you are.

No one knows your child as deeply as you do, and no one loves them like you do. You love your child better, more deeply, and more thoroughly than anyone else. Love is key to helping your child navigate all of life's unique challenges and experiences—including video games. Perhaps your video game rules just haven't worked, and you feel like you are constantly at odds with your children. You might even worry that your lack or excess of concern about video games has done irreparable damage to your children. Parental guilt does not help us or our children; acknowledging our errors and making changes do. I know you are a good parent because you're trying to do both.

Perhaps you need help understanding video games and your child's love of them, help knowing when to put your foot down and when to ease up, or help knowing what to be concerned about and what to let go. You need help understanding the world of video games so that you might know and love thy gamer. If that's you, I have good news for you: you are not alone, and I hope to help.

## Guide Thy Gamer

Hopefully, your situation is not as dire as Tim's. Still, you need help navigating video games with your children. Perhaps the first step toward this end is to admit a truth about your children that you've probably been reticent to admit:

Your kids are gamers.

That's not all they are, of course. They are daughters, sons, students, soccer players, dancers, pianists, friends, and, most important, image-bearers of God. However, you are reading this because, deep down, you know your child is a gamer—it's the one activity he or she seems to enjoy more than any other. Whether you like it or not, video games are really important to your children.

Sometimes this bothers you, though *bother* probably isn't a strong enough word. You fear the games they play are making them more aggressive, rotting their brains, or, at the very least, wasting their time. And if those worries weren't enough, you can't help wondering what life skills they might develop if they would redirect their interests to something more "useful." Other times you think that your child's love of gaming might not be such a big deal—at least your child isn't updating their Tinder profile or using illegal drugs. You might even occasionally enjoy playing games together as a family. And, though you don't like to admit it, when your child is playing games, he or she isn't requiring your attention, which allows you to focus on your own hobbies or knock out tasks around the house. And lots of people play games, right? To be more precise, 214 million Americans play video games regularly,[1] and you may even know a handful of adults in your workplace or at your church who play them and still manage to live productive, happy, God-honoring lives.

There is a good chance you are reading this because you fear your child might be addicted to video games. You've probably been tempted to bring down the hammer and cleanse your home of any device that would play digital games. You may have even tried this a time or two, but your resolve didn't last. Other times, you've seriously considered raising the white flag. Like Tim, you're weary from constantly fighting about video games. You wince every time you tell your children their game time is up because you know how upset you both are about to get. No matter how much screen time you allow, it is never enough to satisfy them, and it's certainly not as much screen time as your child's closest friends get. You know this because they tell you as much every single time you tell them their game time is up. My wife and I are well aware of these two extremes and have considered both. While these extremes might seem to be "easier" solutions, neither serve our children well.

Ridding your home of video games isn't the right tactic because it makes games the enemy. And games, like so many things in God's good world, are wonderful inventions. And like all wonderful inventions, they can be used for good, but they can also be exploited in ways that harm us and those around us. Teaching your children how to navigate wonderful inventions without exploiting themselves and others is one of the most challenging, yet important, jobs God has given you as a parent.

Video games are generally fun and, contrary to what you may have heard in church a time or two, God is not opposed to fun. In fact, God is the author of games and play and fun. Games can also be deeply challenging, imaginative, and adventurous. They provide us opportunities to improve, solve problems, overcome challenges, build friendships, share laughs, and even save the world. And yes, the worlds we save in video games are virtual, but that doesn't mean the quests we complete in them are meaningless. Unlike other forms of media our children consume, games give us agency. We read books and watch shows and movies, but we *play* games. And that interactivity means games are brimming with potential—potential to help us develop perseverance, relieve stress, learn empathy, and cultivate deeper relationships.

It is that potential, however, that makes games ripe for misuse and even abuse. They can be really difficult to put down, and some of the most popular games are deliberately designed to keep impressionable people playing well beyond what is healthy or beneficial. So completely avoiding screen-time limits can be an unloving tactic. Yes, your child will praise you for a time, but their young impressionable minds are not equipped to self-regulate. Unless you have an extremely mentally and emotionally mature child, he or she will likely fail to recognize what an unhealthy relationship with digital gaming looks like. Such unhealthy relationships can hinder your child's development and their interpersonal relationships with you and others. If you let them play games as much as they want, all those potential benefits of video games that we've mentioned will soon be overshadowed by your child's irritability and lack of self-control.

Simply put, video games have tremendous potential, but children need help unlocking that potential and using games for their good, the good of the world, and for the glory of God. Your child also needs you to equip them to fight the temptation to cultivate a selfish, unhealthy, or even destructive relationship with all kinds of media, particularly video games. If this sounds like an insurmountable task, remember that no one in all the world is better equipped than you for this task. Despite what your children might say in the heat of an argument, there is no one they love and respect more than you, and no one loves your children better than you do.

## Love Thy Gamer

If you find yourself regularly thinking, *If my child would just stop playing video games, I'd be a better parent*, then the biggest problem you need to tackle regarding video games lies with you, not your children. You are called to love the children God has given you, not the children you want them to be. And your children need to know that you want to be around them and that you are interested in the things they are interested in. Start there.

The fact that video games are interactive means they engage children on a deeper level than books or television or movies. This doesn't make games more dangerous than other forms of media; it just makes them different. Your children need your help understanding what makes games different so that they can engage them in ways that promote their flourishing. It is always easier to label things as categorically good or bad than it is to understand them. It's easier to label games as either great or awful, a fun hobby or a waste of time, enriching and rewarding or addictive and pointless. Your child's experience can be any of these, but their experience can't be all these things at once. Your children need to know that you care enough about them to take a genuine interest in their hobbies.

Consider this: When was the last time you spoke with your children about the video games they play and their experience playing them? Telling them to turn a game off doesn't count—that's talking *at* your children, not talking *with* them. When was the last time you practiced genuine curiosity and asked your child to describe their favorite game and why they enjoy playing it so much?

Your children's brains are still developing. That means they need help understanding what a healthy relationship with video games looks like. If that feels like an impossible task, know that you are not alone. It feels that way for me too sometimes, but I've been reading and writing about video games and parenting for over a decade. My kids don't have a perfect relationship with video games, but we have made progress. And that's the goal of this book: making progress. With a little bit of effort, video games don't have to be a constant source of contention in your home.

## Understanding Video Games

The human story is one of constant misuse. People take wonderful, compelling things intended to help grow and serve ourselves and our neighbors and wind up using them in ways that damage and exploit instead. In other words, the first step Christian parents should take regarding video games is to make an effort to understand them. We need to understand their strengths and weaknesses, their potential for our good and the good of the world, as well as their potential problem areas and the ways we might be tempted to misuse them to our detriment and the detriment of our neighbors.

We need to cut through the competing headlines about the greatness and dangers of video games to unpack a truly Christian understanding of interactive media. We are going to talk about what makes games great and their many potential benefits to those who play them responsibly. We will unpack the ways children are tempted to cultivate an unhealthy relationship with video games. We will see that video games, like all things in our world, are broken. We will answer questions often posed about video games such as: "Do violent video games make kids more aggressive?" and "How do I know if my child is a video game addict?" and "Aren't video games hotbeds of sexism and misogyny?". We will also spend a chapter navigating the most complicated aspects of parenting gamers: setting screen-time limits, parental controls, and learning how to protect your children online. However, before we tackle these crucial topics, we should acknowledge the elephant in the room: the church has had a poor track record of dealing with video games honestly.

Listen, I get it. I have heard the same things you have at church or from fellow Christian parents: "All my kid wants to do is play *Fortnite,* and when I turn it off, he freaks out!" I have frustrations with my own children too. My wife and I often lament how our eldest daughter would, if given the freedom, do nothing other than play *Roblox*. We all want our children to be kind, thoughtful, resilient, industrious, well rounded, and, most important, godly. We fear that a steady diet of digital gaming will hinder their emotional, intellectual, and spiritual development. The truth about video games, however, is that they aren't quite so easy to label.

While playing games for hours on end can have a negative impact on children, research has shown that, when played in moderation, there are many positive effects of digital gaming, which we will unpack in the next chapter. Still, painting video games in a negative light is what many pastors and church leaders have been doing for some time now. And don't get me wrong, most church leaders don't label games as completely evil; they just can't fathom games being anything more than mindless entertainment.

One of the most popular Christian bloggers, Tim Challies, recently summarized this well: "Let's be honest: there is little intrinsic value in gaming. For most of us it is merely entertainment."[2]

Slightly more on the nose, Mark Driscoll once preached that "video games aren't sinful, they're just stupid."[3] Douglas Wilson believes video games are making kids ignorant.[4] And Peter Leithart once claimed that "if all the gamers devoted just one percent of their gaming hours to something with real-world impact, they could move the world."[5] To be clear, these men are bringing up valid questions despite selectively asking them of video games when they should also be applied to many hobbies: sports (both participation and fandom), television, social media, and novels are just a few that come to mind. Nonetheless, these perspectives on video games illustrate a pattern: in the church, where we are challenged to live for something much bigger than ourselves, we wonder if video games are worth our time and energy at all.

But what does the Bible say about video games? At first glance, we might assume nothing at all since there were no video games in the first century. However, in chapter 2 we will see that video games are a type of play, and the Bible does address the value of play. In this chapter, we will also address some of the inherent values of video games and how we might leverage these values for the glory of God and the good of our neighbors. This brings up another important aspect about video games: they are massively popular and represent a massive opportunity for followers of Jesus.

## The Popularity and Opportunity of Video Games

We live in a world that is giving much of its time, money, and energy to video games, and this isn't likely to change anytime soon:

- According to the Entertainment Software Association's 2020 annual report: 64 percent of U.S. adults and 70 percent of those under eighteen regularly play video games.[6]
- Seventy-five percent of American households are home to at least one person who plays video games regularly.[7]
- In 2017, U.S. video game revenue reached $36 billion (a growth of 18% over 2016).[8]
- In 2013, *Grand Theft Auto V* made over $1 billion in revenue in its first three days of sales.[9]

And who plays games is changing too. Despite what you may have heard, video games are no longer a predominantly young male hobby. My ten-year-old daughter is as committed to *Roblox* as most boys her age are to *Minecraft* or *Fortnite*. It's also worth pointing out that video games are no longer a hobby relegated to children and most gamers are not antisocial:[10]

- The average gamer is thirty-five years old.
- In 2021 women made up 45 percent of all gamers in the United States. This was an increase from 41 percent the previous year.[11]
- Twenty-seven percent of gamers are under the age of eighteen.
- Eighty-three percent of African American teens play video games compared to 71 percent of white teens.[12]
- The most frequent gamers who play multi-player and online games spend an average of 4.6 hours per week playing with others in person.
- Twenty-one percent of gamers play with family members; 15 percent play with their spouse or partner.

These statistics paint a clear picture: we live in a culture of gamers. This is why merely raising the alarm about the potential dangers of video games is an insufficient approach. It is insufficient not only because it fails to acknowledge the good in gaming but also because it neglects the missional opportunity represented in these statistics. If we only view our nation's interest in gaming as a problem to be fixed and fail to see the millions of gamers across the United States as people to be loved, served, and reached, then we aren't looking hard enough.

Full disclosure: I am a gamer and have been for the last thirty years. I have taken breaks from gaming from time to time, but I have always come back. But I can say with confidence that I have a healthy relationship with games. They are a wonderful, yet small, part of my life. I know my limits and exercise self-control. I have other hobbies that I enjoy as much as or more than video games (not that they can't or shouldn't be your primary hobby). Video games are most often a source of joy and connection with others rather than a source of frustration and isolation. But more than that, I have also considered myself a missionary to gamers and nerds for over a decade. For years, I worked part-time for an organization called Gamechurch, a ministry dedicated to bridging the gap between the gospel and the gamer. And a few years ago, along with some like-minded friends, I set out to launch a new nonprofit ministry called Love Thy Nerd,[13] a ministry dedicated to being the love of Jesus to nerds and nerd culture. Part of our mission at Love Thy Nerd is to understand the breadth and depth of "nerd culture." If we really love people, we will make an effort to understand who they are and what they are about. This includes taking an interest in whatever holds their interest.

Jesus didn't just preach to people; He also built relationships. He ate with sinners and tax collectors (Mark 2:13–17) and took a genuine interest in everyone He ministered to. One of the simplest ways you can love your child and build a genuine relationship with them is by making an honest effort to understand their interests and passions. You don't have to have the same level of interest in video games as your child does, not even close. But loving them does mean taking an interest, just as you would if your child was really into soccer or piano or theater. If we only see a preoccupation with video games as a problem to be solved and not an opportunity for relationship, connection, and mission, then we are missing a massive opportunity.

Your child's love of video gaming connects them to a huge mission field they are likely better positioned to reach with the love of Jesus than you are. You can help them engage games in a way that honors God and spreads the good news about Jesus.

So, in addition to unpacking the potential benefits and dangers of digital gaming, I have also dedicated a chapter to embracing and engaging the mission field of digital gaming. We will cover this in the fifth chapter.

Your children need you to help them navigate video games responsibly and *Christianly*, but more than that, they need you to be interested and invested. Video games aren't all good or all bad; they're wonderful, broken, and complicated all at the same time. They can be hyperviolent, misogynistic, and addictive. But they can also be awe-inspiring, community building, and confidence boosting. They're also a lot of fun—and fun is not a value God is opposed to. So let's get rid of our stereotypes, both good and bad, and dig into what games actually are, what they do, and what they can be. Let's also be honest about the key ways we often misuse games. Let's discover what the Bible has to say about games. And finally, I am convinced that if we make the necessary effort to understand and even play video games in a God-honoring way, we will be more than happier and healthier people. We will also be poised to point our children to Jesus and equip them to point others to Him.

# Games Are Good

Thus says the LORD of hosts: Old men and old women
shall again sit in the streets of Jerusalem, each with staff
in hand because of great age. And the streets of the city
shall be full of boys and girls playing in its streets.

ZECHARIAH 8:4–5 ESV

An infant will play beside the cobra's pit, and a toddler
will put his hand into a snake's den. They will not harm
or destroy each other on my entire holy mountain, for the
land will be as full of the knowledge of the LORD as the
sea is filled with water.

ISAIAH 11:8–9

The story of the Bible begins and ends with play. Zechariah's vision
of a renewed world was playful. And according to Isaiah's vision
of God's kingdom, life is more playful where God is known more
deeply. So we should not give in to the idea that games are a waste

of time when Scripture speaks of them as a demonstration of God's goodness. If you have spent much time in church, however, there is a good chance Isaiah's future vision of games isn't easy to accept.

There is a solid possibility that you are reading this book because you think games are a waste of time. You may see *some* value in board games, card games, or sports, but it's difficult for you to see *video* games as one of God's good gifts. You probably fear that your children's interest in video games is hindering their development. Studies have shown, however, that video games in moderation can be good for us. Playing video games can improve children's memory and pattern recognition, teach them problem-solving skills, and improve their fine motor skills.[1]

Additionally, video games can benefit children's self-esteem. When your children are playing video games, they are often winning. They are saving the world, earning trophies and achievements, leveling up, unlocking new features, learning new skills, solving problems, and overcoming obstacles. They are being entertained, engaged, tested, and challenged. Video games are inherently educational; even if the education they are receiving while gaming is relegated primarily to the world of the game, they are still learning. When your children play video games, they are not merely absorbing information. They are actively responding to it. In other words, within the confines of the games they play, your children are typically very productive people. Dr. Jane McGonigal, author and game designer, describes this well:

> Gamers want to know: Where in the real world, is
> that gamer sense of being fully alive, focused, and

engaged in every moment? Where is the gamer feeling of power, heroic purpose, and community? Where are the bursts of exhilarating and creative game accomplishment? Where is the heart-expanding thrill of success and team victory? While gamers may experience these pleasures occasionally in their real lives, they experience them almost constantly when they are playing their favorite video games.[2]

I know what you are thinking: *That all sounds great, but shouldn't we be concerned that our children are having these productive, empowered experiences in digital worlds rather than the real one?* We certainly don't want our children to grow so comfortable in digital spaces that they are ill-equipped to engage meaningfully outside them. Could it be, however, that a responsible relationship with games could actually empower us to engage more purposefully in the real world? If video games really are part of God's good creation, then there is beauty and benefit within them. It is possible to play video games for the glory of God and the good of the world.

The possibility that video games could be played to the glory of God might be difficult to stomach, particularly if video games are all your children want to do or talk about. However, before we unpack the most troubling and challenging aspects of our children's relationship with video games, we need to make an honest effort to understand video games—what they are, what they do, and where their value comes from.

If there is play in the new heavens and new earth, then we should carefully investigate the value of play in God's eyes. What potential do video games possess, as a type of play, for our good and the good of the world? What good is there in video games? The majority of this chapter will answer these questions, but first, we should understand what video games are and how they operate. To do so, we must start with the concept that spawned them: play.

## What Is Play?

Simply put, video games are a type of game, and games are a type of play. So, if we hope to understand some of the potential benefits and values of video games, we need to unpack what play is and why it matters. Stuart Brown, the founder of the National Institute of Play, has intensively studied play and has concluded that it has the power to significantly improve everything from personal health to relationships to education to organizations' ability to innovate.[3] Play "leads to brain plasticity, adaptability, and creativity. . . . Nothing fires up the brain like play."[4] Play is incredibly important to the development of children, but more than that, it is good for adults too. But what is play? Play is anything we do that is intrinsically motivated and engaged for recreational enjoyment.

That intrinsically motivated part is important because some of our richest, most valuable experiences in life are motivated this way. Being intrinsically motivated means not having to offer any kind of tangible reward for your children to play; the experience of play is reward enough. And when I say that play is engaged for recreational enjoyment, I mean its purpose is not to earn money or produce a product. Johan Huizinga, who was a Dutch historian and cultural theorist, is widely considered the father of ludology—the study of games. In his famous book on play, *Homo Ludens* ("the playing man"), Huizinga identified five characteristics that play must have:

1. Play is free; is, in fact, freedom.
2. Play is not "ordinary" or "real" life.
3. Play is distinct from "ordinary" life both as to locality and duration.
4. Play creates order; is order. Play demands order absolute and supreme.
5. Play is connected with no material interest, and no profit can be gained from it.[5]

While Huizinga did not study play from a Christian perspective, I believe his characteristics of play are present on page one of the Bible and very much relate to a Christian worldview.

### *Play is free.*

There is a playfulness to the way God created the universe. It could be argued that God's act of creation in Genesis 1:1 was the most free act in history. God did not create out of obligation, necessity, or loneliness. He created freely. He created because He wanted to and expressed delight in everything He made, declaring it "good." And upon creating human beings in His image, He declared all He made "very good" (Gen. 1:31). The Psalms tell us that God delights in His works (Ps. 104:31) and in His people (Ps. 149:4).

Think about how your children often feel on the playground or even just playing in the backyard. These are moments of glorious freedom—moments whose goodness you've never questioned because they are so instinctively joyful. I believe this is why both Isaiah and Zechariah envisioned a future, renewed world where children can play without fear of harm (Isa. 11:8–9; Zech. 8:4–5).

A friend of mine recently moved to a new neighborhood. But before doing so, she took her five children for one last trip to the park near their old home. She described it like this:

> Tonight was everything my heart needed. Rebecca and Adam, our old neighbors, and their kids met us at the neighborhood park along with my best friend Anna and her kids. Together, our twelve children recruited the other ten plus kids at the playground to play a giant game of "cops and robbers."
>
> It was beautiful. Kids we don't know, kids we've known since birth, children of immigrants, a preteen who started off "too cool for school," little ones who were barely out of diapers, big kids turning thirteen—all of them playing deliberately and meaningfully together for a full hour. They were cheering for each other, working together, and having an absolute blast building a kid kingdom while the parents talked. I loved everything about this park and these people.

On the way home, my son Ezra and I talked about how wonderful it was to have one "last park day" before we moved. I told him it felt like the nearest thing to heaven that I may ever feel here on Earth. It was nothing short of beautiful watching those kids just enjoying the world they built together across boundaries and with complete agreement and full joy.

Modern video games, in their best moments, provide us with digital spaces to have these kinds of almost Eden-like experiences. They are safe places where we can play, experiment, explore, and connect. To be fair, some video games can feel more like work than play, but it should be noted that much of what motivates children to play those games is intrinsic to the game experience itself. You've probably had similar experiences playing video games. Maybe it was the first time you played a 3D game and were delighted at how you could travel in any direction in order to explore an unknown world. Perhaps it was the first time you played a game with a virtual reality (VR) headset and were fascinated by the new possibilities it introduced. Maybe you'd have to go back even further to the first time you ever played a video game. Even if it was something as simple as the original *Super Mario Bros.* or *Pong*, the simple experience of pressing a button and seeing your input play out on a screen was surprising, delightful, and fun.

Don't get me wrong. I think, in many ways, the richest forms of play are experienced in person on actual playgrounds rather than digital ones. I want my children to have playful experiences at parks, in the woods behind our house, and at the swimming pool in the summer. Still, the superiority of actual playgrounds doesn't render digital ones worthless. For example, playing *Minecraft* for the very first time is, for lack of a better word, a magical experience. *Minecraft*'s survival mode throws players into a massive world of mysterious mines, mountains, and creatures that they must learn to tame through exploration and experimentation and community. (Most people share their worlds with friends.) The game can also be breathtakingly beautiful—both in terms of the world players inhabit and of the one they build together with friends. (The things people can and have built in *Minecraft* are truly astounding.) It's an experience I have gotten to experience twice—once through my eyes and once through the eyes of my oldest daughter.

### *Play is not "ordinary" or "real" life.*

The freedom to explore and experiment in video games comes to us on a level that is set apart from the pressures of our workweek and unhindered by the need to produce. While Genesis 1:31 marks the end of the work of creation, creation isn't truly complete until God gives His people the gift of rest by modeling it on the seventh day.

Play is much closer to rest than work. We play not to survive but because we want to. We feel a binding necessity to work, but we play because it makes us happy. Sometimes work is enjoyable, but we also know that work is cursed. Sometimes we work, and others get to enjoy the fruit of our labors more than we do. Sometimes we work, and, despite our best efforts, things don't go according to plan. Sometimes we work, and the process seems to take more from us than it gives. Genesis 3:17–19, post fall, describes work as painful toil and the fruit it produces as restricted by thorns and thistles. We shouldn't be surprised that biblical prophets like Isaiah envisioned a renewed heavenly future where God's people get to enjoy the benefits of the work of their hands (Isa. 65:22).

Even though play is free and set apart from real life, it is important to recognize that playgrounds can be dangerous places. Every child faces temptation on the playground—temptation to cheat, to be selfish, to lose bitterly and win mercilessly. Playgrounds are also places where we can be hurt by others. When my kids play with each other or with other kids on our block, someone inevitably gets hurt. The hurt experienced there can be physical (i.e., scraped knees) or emotional (i.e., bullying or exclusion). The presence of these temptations does not diminish the value of play but rather demonstrates that play has tremendous potential while simultaneously being deeply broken. This is why Zechariah and Isaiah envisioned a coming day when children will play in dangerous places without fear—on streets and over the holes of snakes (Zech. 8:4–5; Isa. 11:8–9).

In the meantime, while we await the day when we can play without fear of harm, our children need our help to learn to play well.

### Play is distinct from "ordinary" life both as to locality and duration.

Play is cursed in its own unique ways that we will unpack in the next chapter, but for now, it is important to note how play is set apart from work. Sometimes we play in ways that possess some elements of work; however, play in its purest form is always free from the pressures of survival. It is also set apart in terms of rules. When we enter into play, we agree to abide by explicit or implied rules, which are often different to those we normally follow. This is why Huizinga referred to play as "the magic circle." He wasn't trying to say that there is anything mystical about play but, rather, that it is unique and that it has been hugely influential in the development of human culture and institutions:

> All play moves and has its being within a play-ground marked off beforehand either materially or ideally, deliberately or as a matter of course. Just as there is no formal difference between play and ritual, so the "consecrated spot" cannot be formally distinguished from the play-ground. The arena, the card-table, the magic circle, the temple, the stage, the screen, the tennis court, the court of justice, etc, are all in form and function play-grounds, i.e. forbidden spots, isolated, hedged round, hallowed, within which special rules obtain. All are temporary worlds within the ordinary world, dedicated to the performance of an act apart.[6]

Playgrounds give opportunities to take a break from the "real" world and participate in a new shared world we are actively creating with other people. They are places where we learn creative problem-solving and develop social skills. Games provide children with safe places to develop their character, cultivate teamwork, and learn how to both win and lose. The dangers of playgrounds, however, also apply to video games but don't diminish their potential. If you caught your child cheating in a soccer match, you wouldn't blame soccer. You'd talk to your children about playing by the rules and the value of honor and honesty. Your children need you to model for them how to play well—in a way that prioritizes love of God and neighbor.

### *Play creates order; is order. Play demands order absolute and supreme.*

In Genesis 1:2, the earth is described as "without form and void" (ESV). The idea here is that the earth was not yet fruitful or beneficial. It is not that it wasn't good, but it was empty. Similar language is used in the Bible to describe a desert. The remainder of Genesis 1 is dedicated to God bringing order and beauty to an empty, uncultivated world. The vegetation, the light, and the day/night cycle all contribute to making a world that is beneficial to human beings. In other words, God took a desert-like place and provided the systems, structures, and guidance necessary to make it good *for us*.

Games are structured forms of play, being one among many ways we mirror God's work of bringing order to our world. When kids play games in the park with kids they've just met, they bring order and beauty to that place for their own benefit and the benefit of those around them. When we play games with others, we join together in the shared work of developing rules that have the potential to make the playground a better place for those inhabiting it. Everyone playing a game has a vested interest in creating and sustaining an equitable experience; games simulate and incentivize responsible engagement with the world and with others. In other words, playing games is one of the many ways we can live out our identity as God's image-bearers.

Games provide safe places for us to learn and grow. If we can teach our children to play well, games can act as simulations that send them out with a strategy to make their world and the world of those around them better. Now, your children will certainly be tempted to play games in ways that ignore the needs or diminish the humanity of their neighbors. However, many modern video games allow players the freedom to make a wide array of moral decisions. While this freedom means that players could choose to do evil within the game, most game worlds possess a clear sense of justice where doing evil comes with clear and often severe consequences. In other worlds, video games tend to encourage heroic or selfless actions over evil or selfish actions. For example, in the *Dishonored* series, players can choose to complete missions violently or nonviolently, but the former results in the game world becoming increasingly dark and dangerous. Such depictions of the consequences of selfish actions are not unlike many instructive stories in the Bible—like how 2 Samuel unfolds the devastating consequences of David's choice to commit adultery with Bathsheba and have her husband killed.

## Play is connected with no material interest.

God rested on the seventh day, setting a precedent for those made in His image (Gen. 2:2). We are not only encouraged to rest but commanded to (Exod. 20:8–11). The Sabbath reminds us that

God's vision for human flourishing involves not only work but also rest. And to be more specific, God calls us to rest in such a way that we cease from being productive. We are to deliberately take a break from producing food or making money. God rested from His work—from carefully ordering the world for the betterment of people. In a world where so many people have second jobs and side hustles, taking time to play is more important than ever. It may not seem important for your children who probably get much more playtime than you, but it is important for you both.

Research on the benefits of playing games bears this out. Play helps children improve their communication and social skills. Playing games helps kids develop understanding of social rules, build friendships, learn to share, practice patience and perseverance, grow in empathy, and cultivate a sense of belonging.[7] Playing games, however, is not only good for kids; it also benefits parents. Playing games helps relieve stress, improves brain function, stimulates the mind, boosts creativity, improves your relationships, and keeps you feeling young and energetic.[8]

Most of us don't play games to make money or get ahead. We play games because we want to. And because we generally don't play games for selfish gain, games have the potential to draw us closer to others. When we play games, we aren't trying to sell anything, so playing games with others presents us with opportunities to demonstrate that we value them beyond mutual gain and favors. The experience of playing together is itself the reward.

It is worth noting that there are people who play video games today in ways that are motivated by financial gain. The most notable examples are esports players (professional video gamers) and streamers (people who broadcast their video game play live on websites like Twitch). In 2018, Twitch reported 2.2 million active broadcasters who earned nearly 15 million viewers a day.[9] The most successful streamers on Twitch make hundreds of thousands of dollars and approach streaming as a full-time job. However, it is important to note that very few people can earn a living wage playing video games. There is a good chance, however, that your children dream of being one of the select few who get paid to play video games full-time. If that's you, I encourage you to read Jonathan Clauson's article, "Should I Quit My Job and Stream Video Games All Day?" to help you understand the world of streaming and equip you to provide your children with a much-needed reality check.[10] The reality is that the more job-like your approach to gaming is, the less restful and truly playful it will become. Our time playing games is most memorable and beneficial when the reward is the experience itself.

## What Are Video Games?

Now that we have established what play is and why it is valuable, let's unpack the type of play you bought this book to better understand—video games. What are they and what makes them unique?

What comes to mind when you think of video games? Perhaps you think of graphic violence or mindless entertainment. You might assume your children's obsession with video games borders on addiction. These things are not intrinsic to video games, but they are aspects of our experience, which do not necessarily give us a clear definition of what video games are. It is all too easy to let our strongest negative experiences shape our understanding of something. There are plenty of graphically violent video games and plenty of children with unhealthy relationships with gaming, but this is far from an accurate picture of what games are or what they can be in your home with proper guidance and boundaries. In other words, we need to remind ourselves that video games aren't inherently evil.

If God is the author of play, then our worst experiences with video games are examples of our human potential to corrupt God's good creation. Consider drugs, for instance, which can be used to treat the sick or even save them from death, and yet others sell drugs to minors, preying on their lack of self-control and ushering them into addiction. Similarly, the presence of graphic violence and the presence of addictive elements can mask the positive potential of video games. If your child already has an unhealthy relationship with video games or plays video games with dark or violent content, chances are you struggle to see much potential for good in them. If that's you, I want to challenge you to look past the worst in video games and make an effort to truly understand them and their potential. We don't have to love video games or even play them ourselves; however, loving our children well should motivate us to strive for an accurate understanding of the things they most enjoy. To understand the potential of video games, we must set aside our preconceived notions and make an effort to understand them at face value. So, what are video games at the most fundamental level?

Video games are digital forms of structured play governed by rules and objectives. Like other forms of media, video games tell stories, but they communicate their narratives through play. And remember, play is one of God's good gifts. Games have inherent value and can be engaged in ways that lead to flourishing. This definition highlights four aspects of video games that are important to understanding them: they are accessible, interactive, social, and tell stories through play.

### Video games are accessible.

Video games are not lesser forms of play because they are digital. Their digital nature makes them more accessible than many other forms of play. The mental and social benefits of playing some video games may be less pronounced than playing games on a playground or playing a team sport, but that does not mean they are inherently inferior. In fact, video games can provide us with unique experiences we can't have in the "real" world. For example, you are unlikely to team up with friends to save the world from an alien invading force this week. Your kids might simulate a similar experience with their imaginations in the park or on your block, but such experiences take a lot more doing: they'd need access to friends willing and able to play and safe space within which to play. To give an even more accessible example, you aren't likely to play tackle football for the Dallas Cowboys this week either. Both experiences are readily available to us in video games. Video games also give people who physically cannot do things like play football a taste of the experience. And with the vast majority of American households possessing devices on which games can be played, it is clear that video games provide more attainable and available places to experience the many benefits of play.

## *Video games are interactive.*

One of the most common mistakes parents make regarding video games is to lump them in with all other types of screen time like watching TV or scrolling through social media. This isn't to say that you shouldn't limit the amount of video game time you allow your children each day but, rather, to point out that your children's experience playing video games is distinctly different.

When your children play video games, they aren't just consuming information; they are making decisions and solving problems. When your children play games with friends, they are often building leadership skills and learning teamwork. When they fail to win a game or complete a level, they are learning from their mistakes and developing resilience. You may not feel like their time playing video games is productive, but it is important to recognize that it feels productive to your kids. In a recent study by Brigham Young University information systems, professors found that "playing video games for 45 minutes with coworkers can improve productivity by 20 percent."[11] It is important to note that the games chosen were games agreed to require team coordination, but this nevertheless demonstrates how playing certain video games for the right amount of time can serve as a warm-up for a better, more productive day.

Bottom line: video games are different from other types of media. When your kids play them, their minds are being engaged on a far more active level than they are when they are watching television or scrolling through Instagram or TikTok. And more often than not, they are doing those things alongside or against other players.

### *Video games are social.*

Even if your child mostly plays single-player games, they are likely interacting with others in those games in our highly connected digital world. They might be streaming their single-player experience and interacting with those who are watching, or they might be trying to beat a friend's high score or best time. At the very least, they have friends who see what they are playing and vice versa. They check in with those friends later and build stronger bonds because of it.

Online games also provide us opportunities to make new connections, and the more deeply and consistently we play, the more meaningful those connections can become. This is, understandably, a scary proposition for many parents and is not one that I am advocating for all children. Like anything else we do online, we need to keep careful watch on those our kids are interacting with and how. That said, there are instances in which your children might play games with new friends in ways that improve their relationships. I personally recommend only allowing your children to voice chat with other kids she or he knows. Most gaming systems have parental controls that allow you to set limitations on who your child can interact with. Additionally, most gaming systems allow parents to set time limits and block access to games with adult themes. Still, you might be surprised to see how the problem-solving and teamwork required in many games may help them develop closer bonds with friends they once found themselves at odds with. Playing video games connects your children to others in settings outside the games they play. Part of why they love video games is the shared vocabulary they develop with friends who play the same games and the sense of belonging that comes with it.

## *Video games tell stories through play.*

Video game stories are not traditional narratives. Unlike reading a novel or watching a film, the story of a video game is one in which the player participates. Video games combine traditional forms of storytelling with interactive gameplay. Game designer Clint Hocking, lead designer on *Far Cry 2*, *Splinter Cell*, and *Watch Dogs: Legion*, describes the story of games as a "ludonarrative," a term that combines ludology (the study of games) and narrative (story).[12] Many games today have strong cinematic elements with beautiful cutscenes and voice acting from high-profile actors, but these cinematic elements only tell a small part of their stories. A game's story unfolds in the interactive play experience, which, depending on the game, can be linear (on a set path) or open to how players can shape the world and story through their actions. But even in linear experiences, the players' input into the system can play heavily into the narrative they experience. Everything from the buttons they press to the number of times they fail to complete a level to the way they solve problems contributes to the unfolding ludonarrative. Consequently, game designers often speak of the stories of games as emergent narratives, meaning the designers themselves can't entirely predict the story players will experience because of player behavior and game elements that are randomly generated. The story line players experience may not be written into the game by its developers, but it is one that emerges as players interact with the game's world and systems.

While a particular game might have an expertly crafted world, the story cannot be encapsulated merely in the prologue and conclusion. Part of why your children, or anyone else, enjoys playing video games is because their input matters. Their decisions make a difference. And even though these narratives can hook your children in ways that might distract them from interacting meaningfully in the real world, the stories that play out in video games are ones in which our contribution is honored, valued, and rewarded. There is a parable here about how we interact with our children and how we personally value their input in our families, but for now, it is important to acknowledge how video games tell stories because they are full of potential for our good and the good of the world.

## What Good Are Video Games?

Now that we have unpacked the power of play and defined what video games are, we must tackle the question of what value they bring to our lives. There are numerous inherent values to video games, more than we have time to tackle, but here are a few. Let's start with the most obvious:

### Fun

Remember what Tim Challies said? "There is little intrinsic value in gaming. For most of us it is merely entertainment."[13] I take issue with this statement for a couple of reasons. First, there are many intrinsic values of video games. We shouldn't be surprised when games *feel* like a waste of time when we haven't bothered to consider what those values might be. Second, fun isn't an inferior value to education or productivity. Remember, we serve a wonderfully creative God who created games and fun. Our God created us not only to work and be productive but to rest and to play.

Johan Huizinga wrote that the primary aspect of play is that it is fun—it's enjoyable.[14] What did God say of everything He made in the garden? It was good. God did not just make a world that would be useful but also one that would be enjoyable to His creatures, particularly those made in His image. Furthermore, God wove into creation a rhythm of rest. He commanded Adam and Eve not only to work and keep the garden but to take a day and cease from work and productivity. So while games might not seem like the most productive use of our time, it is important that we make time for being unproductive and not always equate it with laziness.

Isaiah's vision of the new heavens and new earth is one in which people build houses and live in them and plant vineyards and enjoy their fruit (Isa. 65:21). In other words, the new heaven is not only a place where we are productive but also a place where we get to rest and enjoy the fruit of our hard work. For many, video games are their way of unwinding and rewarding themselves with some fun after a productive day. Your children probably are not as productive as you are, but you shouldn't expect them to be—they are children, after all. However, some dedicated gaming time can be a valuable reward for your children after they have had a productive day of their own in which they finished chores, practiced piano, went to soccer practice, and did their homework.

## *Beauty*

Video games are made by people who were fearfully and wonderfully made in the image of God (Ps. 139:14), people who, by their very nature, reflect God's beauty and goodness. We should not be surprised when digital worlds take our breath away. Nor should we be alarmed when digital spaces appear more interesting than our own. We should guard against the temptation to become so wrapped up in these worlds that we neglect more pressing duties in the real world; however, it is also important to remember that the Bible encourages us to imagine a better world (Rev. 21:1–4; Isa. 65:17–25)—one that is just and fair and beautiful (Rev. 21:9–11). Video games have the potential to astonish us, spark our curiosity, and even help us cultivate a vision for a better world.

Part of the reason people tend to enjoy game worlds is because, in many ways, they are better than our own. We live in a world where wicked people escape consequences of unjust actions while the innocent are oppressed. Video games, however, are almost always fair; their worlds are built on absolute rules that come with immediate and just consequences. Remember that video games are digital forms of structured play. They are governed by rules that all players must obey. And while it is possible to cheat or hack some video games, this is the exception, not the rule. Most video games preclude cheating, and most multiplayer games bring all players into the game world on equal footing by creating balance and rewarding skill rather than luck. In other words, the game worlds your children visit give them a small picture of the kind of world

God calls us to strive to create in our homes, our churches, and our culture—a world that is just and fair and rewarding.

One of the most common complaints I hear parents make about video games, my wife included, is that their children so often seem to have a bad attitude after playing. Your children may even seem listless or unenthused about everything else the day holds once their time playing video games has ended. Truth be told, saving the world, building an empire, or winning the Super Bowl will almost always be more exciting than unloading the dishwasher, eating dinner, and doing your homework. The fact that normal life is less exhilarating than video games shouldn't surprise us; this further illustrates their potential. We will unpack strategies for helping your children to not see everything else they do in a day as a letdown and discuss how to help your children cultivate other hobbies in chapter 4.

## *Community*

Video games bring people together. This idea likely bothers you because, after all, you grew up building community with people in physical spaces like your church or school. Today's teenagers, often referred to as Generation Z, grew up with smartphones and social media. They've never known a world where they did not have 24/7 instant access to friends, family, work, media, and information.[15] Your children are growing up in a different world than you did. I am not suggesting that you give them free rein of the internet or social media—I personally recommend holding off letting your children have social media accounts as long as possible—but I am suggesting that the way older children tend to socialize today is vastly different from any other point in human history. And in this strange and often frustrating climate, video games are actually something of a breath of fresh air. Video games provide us with meaningful shared experiences in a world that is growing more and more isolated.[16]

Most multiplayer games train us to work together and to lean on one another's strengths to solve problems. They also often help us understand one another. If you want to know what people are really like, try playing a game with them. You will see how they act under pressure, what they'll do to win, and how they respond to unexpected challenges. Playing video games with your children has been shown to have a positive impact on adolescent development and long-term family outcomes.[17] Video games provide opportunities to open conversations with your teenagers. Even if you can't bring yourself to play games with your children, you can talk to them about the games they play. If you have trouble getting a word out of your children, try asking them about their favorite game, and it's likely you won't be able to get them to shut up. This conversation might not be interesting to you, but your interest in your children and the attempt to enter their world on their terms with a determination to love them will mean everything to them.

When you play games with your children—particularly games whose rules you don't know and whose worlds you are unfamiliar with—the tables are turned. You become the student, and your child becomes the teacher. These are moments of vulnerability and care outside your comfort zone. When you do this, you are stepping into a world that is foreign to you but familiar to your children. Offer to play video games with your children and watch their eyes light up at the prospect of sharing one of their most prized hobbies with one of the people they treasure most. Don't worry if you aren't any good; that's not the point. The goal is a shared, interactive experience. If you are terrible at games, playing them with your children is an opportunity for you to model humility, attentiveness, and perseverance. Again, even if you can't bring yourself to play video games with your kids, you can still build community around them by simply and genuinely asking your children questions. Expressing genuine curiosity about your children's interests, even if you dislike those interests, is one of the simplest ways you can show love to your children.

## *Education and Development*

Playing video games helps us develop critical-thinking and problem-solving skills, which, in turn, helps us be happier, more productive people. Video games are inherently educational. Every time we play games, we learn something about the world, ourselves, or even just about the game itself. They also give us insight into different cultures since they are created by people all over the globe.[18] Further, when we play games with others, we must learn how to handle losing and how to win graciously; video games can teach us humility.[19] Sometimes they can even expose us, forcing us to admit unhealthy attitudes or preconceived notions we have about others. There has even been a recent trend in game design to make what are called "empathy games." Because games are interactive, they have the potential to give us a unique view into the worlds of people who are very different from us—an experience which has the potential to help us grow and even move us to love and serve others more effectively and with greater understanding.

In contrast to violent, over-the-top games like *Call of Duty* and *Grand Theft Auto*, there are also games like *That Dragon, Cancer*; *Papers, Please*; *This War of Mine*; and *Papo & Yo*. *That Dragon, Cancer* puts the player in control of parents whose four-year-old son is suffering from terminal brain cancer and asks the player to care for him. In *Papers, Please*, the player is an immigration officer who examines people's paperwork to determine whether or not to allow entrance to refugees. *This War of Mine* puts the player in control of civilians trying to survive rather than soldiers attempting to conquer. This unique war game was inspired by *One Year in Hell*, an anonymous memoir written by someone who lived through a siege in Bosnia during the 1990s. *Papo & Yo* is an atmospheric puzzle game that uses symbolism to give players a window into the nature of the creator's relationship with his alcoholic father. Obviously, some of these games tackle some rather dark subject matter. I don't share any of these examples to suggest that you or your children play them because that's your job as a parent to determine. I merely bring up these games to point out that video games can give us unique opportunities to see the world from another person's perspective in a way that possesses the potential to help us understand and love our neighbors better.

### Truth

Because games are designed by people made in God's image, we should expect them to reflect His truth. As with everything else in creation, games reflect truth imperfectly. However, if we play with discernment, they can deepen our perspective of, appreciation for, and engagement with the real world.

Games often provide safe spaces where players can grapple with difficult moral decisions. Role-playing video games like *Fallout*, *Skyrim*, and *Mass Effect* not only challenge players to engage in moral decision-making but also allow players to experience some of the consequences of their decisions. And while there are certainly games that require players to engage in sinful and destructive behavior, like the *Grand Theft Auto* series, most games encourage players toward heroism. More often than not, when your children play video games, they are protecting the innocent, advocating for the less fortunate, or fighting against the forces of evil in the world. Video games tend to present players with a rather optimistic view of the world, and while this view is naive in many ways, followers of Jesus should see good in it. Video games often give us a space in which we can efficiently and effectively save the world and make it a better place. We should not, therefore, be surprised to find those who play them feeling encouraged to engage the real world with a greater sense of hope.

### Health

While we were created in the image of God, it is important to recognize that we are physical creatures. Scripture tells us that our physical bodies are temples of the Holy Spirit (1 Cor. 6:19–20). We should, therefore, take an interest in caring for them, and video games can help us do this.[20] Video games have also been shown to improve brain function, concentration, memory, and pattern recognition.[21] Still, these benefits dip significantly when we play for three or more hours a day.[22] To truly tap into the health benefits of gaming, we must play responsibly.

Dr. Andrew Przybylski, psychologist and director of the Oxford Internet Institute, has extensively studied the impact of video games on children's development:[23]

> [There] are good reasons to think that electronic games, like traditional forms of play, have beneficial aspects that set them apart from non-interactive media entertainment. Games provide a wide range of novel cognitive challenges, opportunities for exploration, relaxation, and socialization with peers. Research focusing on the potential benefits of games indicates they may bolster adjustment by providing psychologically rewarding experiences that dispel negative affect,[24] inspire prosocial behavior,[25] foster creativity,[26] as well as broaden self-concept[27] and build social connections.[28]

Video games also give children opportunities to improve and win. When played in moderation, they can improve children's self-esteem.

So while the foundational value of video games is certainly fun, there is much more going on in this medium than might be readily apparent. This is not to say that you should let your children engage video games however they see fit, but video games, in moderation, can be meaningful to your life and your children's lives. So pay attention to what your children are doing: what they play, how often, and how they conduct themselves while playing. But more than that, strive to help them develop a relationship with gaming that recognizes what is good, true, and beautiful while limiting what's most troubling.

Don't just set boundaries. Ask questions. Involve your children in the process of weighing the benefits and drawbacks of differing levels of engagement with different games. And when your children want to talk to you about the games they are playing, don't deflect or ignore them. When your children talk to you about the games they play, they are bidding for your attention—which they deserve by nature of being your children whom you love. So listen, ask follow-up questions, and strive to learn about what they are playing and why it matters to them.

And finally, play games with them. Don't just parent with the On/Off switch. Gaming together provides countless opportunities for teaching and bonding. Perhaps you and your teen might even host game nights for friends and neighbors or attend a gaming convention together. Play responsibly with discernment and moderation. Then dig deeper; ask the Lord to open our eyes to the values of video games that we've failed to see. We may just become more self-aware, more mindful of our neighbors, and more in love with our God.

# Games Are Broken

While video games brim with potential to fill our hearts with wonder, teach us teamwork, challenge us to be more empathetic, and give us an outlet for restful fun, you're probably not feeling quite so optimistic. You might be reading this book because that potential feels overshadowed by a whole lot of junk. While video games are part of God's good creation, they are subject to the same limitations that face all good things: human misuse and abuse. This can come in the form of how people engage them because we can take a game that could be a source of community and fun and instead play so much that we neglect everything else or even treat the people around us as obstacles to more playtime. This can also come in the form of the games themselves. Not all games are created equal. And like films or books, games can feature content that's questionable at best and outright objectifying and dehumanizing at worst.

When I first started researching and writing about video games, the biggest area of concern parents had about them was violence.

Today that has changed. Now, the concern I hear brought up most often by parents is addiction or overuse. There are countless parents who are concerned about the amount of time their children spend playing video games and some that are even worried that their children might actually be clinically addicted. Concerns about violence, however, have not gone away or been completely solved. There are also reasons to be concerned about misogyny, sexual content, and online safety. So in this chapter, we are going to unpack the areas of video gaming that feel really broken. The goal here is to equip you to see clearly. We'll focus on what you should be concerned about and what fears you can let go of by taking a closer look at the biggest problem areas regarding video games.

## Violence and Addiction

On Saturday, August 25, 2018, David Katz, a twenty-four-year-old gamer from Baltimore, walked into the GLHF Game Bar in Jacksonville, Florida, with a pistol and opened fire on those gathered for a *Madden 19* tournament.[1] *Madden* is the leading NFL video game from Electronic Arts. Katz killed two people and wounded nine others before turning the pistol on himself and ending his own life. Katz was allegedly motivated by rage after having been eliminated from the tournament. What made this incident unique from other shootings was its clear connection to video games. For many, this confirmed a direct link between games and real-world violence. Furthermore, Katz was a competitive *Madden* player who had won a few big tournaments and even considered himself one of the best players in the world. Such high-level play requires consistent practice and a tremendous investment of time. This one event was proof to many that the two greatest problems with video games—violence and addiction—were finally taking their toll.

Prior to this tragic event, discussions of violent video games had largely gone silent. This changed in the aftermath of the Marjory Stoneman Douglas High School shooting in Parkland, Florida. At the time, it was the deadliest school shooting within the last five years.[2] A neighbor alleged that gunman Nikolas Cruz played violent video games upwards of fifteen hours a day.[3] In response to "renewed interest in the gun safety debate," President Trump began speaking out against violent video games and media.[4] He eventually met with members of Congress, video game executives, media watchdogs, and a mother from the Parents Television Council to "discuss violent video-game exposure and the correlation to aggression and desensitization in children."[5]

Around this same time, the American Psychiatric Association and the World Health Organization made headlines for similar reasons. The former identified internet gaming disorder as a possible psychiatric illness, and the latter added "Gaming Disorder" to the 11th International Classification of Diseases (ICD-11)—the premier international tool for diagnosing diseases.[6] Combine these events with the recent GamerGate movement (which has resulted in the targeted harassment of numerous women[7] in the gaming industry) and children's obsession with *Fortnite*,[8] and it seems that the game industry's darkest demons are being exposed.[9]

Looking at these incidents on their face, we might conclude that video games are obsessed with violence, addiction, and toxicity. But what is the connection between violent video games and real-world

aggression? As renewed image-bearers, do video games have any
place in the lives of Christ-followers? In our politically charged culture, it can be difficult to get to the bottom of the actual impact of
virtual violence or how concerned we should be about video game
addiction. So let's attempt to set our desire to score political points
aside for a moment and take an honest look at what we currently
know about gaming's greatest demons: violence and addiction.

## Violence

Hundreds of studies have been conducted in recent years to
determine if there is a significant connection between real-world
violence and playing violent video games. When digging into the
research, it seems the jury is still out: there is no real consensus
among researchers on the actual impact of virtual violence on real-
world aggressive behavior.[10]

The most recent study to cite a connection between violent
video games and aggression is a meta-analysis of twenty-four studies on the impact of violent video games. This study reported that
playing violent video games led to increased physical aggression
over time.[11] However, Patrick Markey, professor of psychology at
Villanova University, who has studied video game violence extensively, said that the new findings point to a minor influence of video
games at most, as it "suggests that less than 1 percent of the variance
in aggression [among kids] is explained by exposure to video game
violence."[12] Markey disputed this study's claims about researchers'
consensus on game violence, citing a 2017 study in which only 15
percent of researchers believe that violent games contribute to serious physical aggression in kids.

We live in a deeply politically divided world, and our perceptions of events like school shootings are no less politically influenced. Kerry Shawgo points out: "Finding research to support whatever ideas you already have about video games is easy. . . . There is often little difference between those wishing to implicate or vindicate video games."[13] In the wake of school shootings, for instance, the reactions from liberals and conservatives are disturbingly predictable. The former will decry the lack of regulation on semiautomatic guns, and the latter will decry the prevalence of violent media, particularly video games.

Actually, only about 20 percent of school shooters play violent video games compared to 70 percent of high school students.[14] And despite President Trump's concern about desensitization, studies increasingly show that violent television does not desensitize viewers to actual violence,[15] and players of violent video games show no less ability to differentiate between real and virtual violence.[16] This isn't to say that violent video games aren't a problem, but we would be wise to place them in proper perspective so that we might take the most meaningful steps forward.

*Should you play violent video games?* This lack of consensus among researchers does not mean violent video games have no impact on those who play them. What it really means is that the jury is still out. It is important to remember that video games are a relatively new medium whose impact on us has only been studied for a couple of decades, which is a pretty small window of time when it comes to such research. Given what we know, we should let go of the idea that video games are anything close to the primary culprit of making passive children violent. What motivates children to significant acts of violence and aggression is far more complex and is related more directly to their environment and care than anything else. However, current research does not free us to say violent video games are not a problem for our children. In his article, "Should You Play Violent Video Games?" Kevin Schut, author of *Of Games and God*, said:

> Logic dictates that game violence is likely to have some effect. I mean, if we think games are great teaching tools (and they are!), why would we assume that stops with violence? We humans are story-making creatures. If we constantly engage in stories where people are constantly enemies, stories where the solution to problems is forceful destruction, how can that not shape our way of thinking at least a little?[17]

The mere presence of violence in media is not inherently problematic. Context is key. The Bible, after all, contains numerous instructive stories of graphic violence (i.e., the cross of Christ). Truthfully, most virtual violence is not primarily meant to be redemptive or even instructive but, rather, motivated by entertainment or competition. The story lines of video games often have players engaging in acts of violence to protect the innocent, but even then, what is motivating most players is entertainment—which is drastically different from the violence found in the Bible. There are a few violent games that tell a more nuanced story. Games like *Shadow of the Colossus*[18] artfully illustrate the destructive nature of selfish violence, and *Spec Ops: The Line* is a war game that is brutally honest about the cost of war.[19] While the former might be worth checking out for older children, I certainly wouldn't recommend the latter for anyone under the age of seventeen. I simply bring up these two examples to say that there has been an effort among some game designers to speak more truthfully about the destructive nature of violence.

Additionally, there are literally thousands of wonderful nonviolent video games you and your children can enjoy. That said, many of the largest game franchises contain what most people would consider graphic violence. As a parent, educate yourself on the kinds of content your child might encounter in some of video games' biggest franchises like *Call of Duty*, *Far Cry*, and *Assassin's Creed*. I will share more ideas on how you can educate yourself in the next chapter, but I encourage you to talk to your kids about what they are doing in any violent games you allow.

The fact that current research doesn't compute with headlines like "Study Confirms Link between Violent Video Games and Physical Aggression"[20] and "Little by Little, Violent Video Games Make Us More Aggressive"[21] does not mean we shouldn't be wary of violence in the media our children engage. The violence found in every game tells a story. And much like television and film violence, video game stories are often misleading. Real-world violence is rarely productive, and war is far more complex morally than our favorite media often indicates. If we are going to consume violent media of any kind, we need to give critical thought to it. Violent video games, after all, are products of an already violent culture—a culture in which Christ calls us to be salt and light and to love our neighbors as ourselves.[22]

We are all probably more impacted by our culture's obsession with violence and aggression than we might think. Remember the story I shared about my friend Tim who smashed his son's Nintendo DS? This was a violent response to his son's interest in video games. When we blow up at our children over video games or belittle them for their lack of other interests, we are contributing to a culture of volatility in our homes. And while we might think we are yelling to get our children's attention, such aggressive behavior hinders our relationship with our children. So don't be quick to assume your child's temper is due solely to gaming habits. Refuse to meet their aggression with your aggression. As the most influential adult in the lives of your children, it is your job to set an appropriate and loving tone in how you handle conflict.

So, should you let your children play violent video games? The short answer is no, at least not graphically violent video games when they are young. We will talk about this in the next chapter, but I believe it is really important to pay attention to the ESRB rating of the games your children want to play before you let them play them. Based on current research, it is also important for you to know that if you have let your children play graphically violent games that are not age appropriate, you almost certainly have not turned them into violent monsters. If you regret some of the games you've let your children play, it's not too late to reassert yourself into their gaming habits. At the very least, you can start having critical conversations with your children about the kinds of games they play, what they do in them, and how that relates to their place and actions in day-to-day life.

Every child is different, so I can't give a one-size-fits-all recommendation, but it is easier than ever before to research what kind of content is contained in video games. A little bit of research goes a long way in helping your children play age-appropriate games.

### *Addiction*

The ICD-11 (International Classification of Diseases) defines gaming disorder as:

> a pattern of gaming behavior ("digital-gaming" or "video-gaming") characterized by impaired control over gaming, increasing priority given to gaming over other activities to the extent that gaming takes precedence over other interests and daily activities, and continuation or escalation of gaming despite the occurrence of negative consequences.[23]

The inclusion of gaming disorder in ICD-11 is significant for two reasons. First, because the ICD is not updated very often—the last time prior was 1990. Second, health professionals around the world use the ICD in making decisions about health care and research. The best possible outcome of the inclusion of gaming disorder is that it will lead to more research into how people become addicted and how best to treat addiction. The downside is that many researchers feel that the WHO's decision was premature and may induce unnecessary moral panic.[24] In 2020, nearly thirty academics and mental health professionals wrote a paper opposing the gaming disorder classification,[25] claiming "there was a lack of consensus among researchers who study games and that the quality of the evidence base was low."[26]

*How many gamers are actually addicted?* A recent study comparing gambling addiction with gaming found that 2.6 percent of those aged eighteen to twenty-four and 1 percent of adults in the general population said they had experienced symptoms linked by the researchers with a gambling disorder.[27] One of the earliest studies on game addiction found that nearly 9 percent of gamers age eight to eighteen were addicted to games.[28] On closer inspection, however, this study's negative effects of gaming were far too broad to be helpful. Andrew Przybylski, a psychologist at the Oxford Internet Institute, says this is a common problem in research on gaming addiction.[29] The research that cites the highest numbers of game addicts collects data from support groups or forums where people post about being addicted to gaming. Przybylski says, "It's like asking, 'what is the prevalence of heroin?' and then going to a clean needle exchange and running your survey there." Przybylski cites studies that report less than .5 percent of gamers are addicted. Dr. David Greenfield, founder of The Center for Internet and Technology Addiction, said the figure is likely closer to 1 percent.[30]

It is not difficult to see how misleading headlines like "Playing Games as Addictive as Heroine" might lead to a premature diagnosis.[31] While neuroscientists have pointed out that the areas in the brain associated with the pleasures of drug use are the same as those associated with the pleasures of playing video games, this isn't particularly helpful on a practical level. Christopher J. Ferguson, a professor of psychology at Stetson University, and Patrick Markey, a professor of psychology at Villanova, point out: "These areas of the brain—those that produce and respond to the neurotransmitter dopamine—are involved in just about any pleasurable activity: having sex, enjoying a nice conversation, eating good food, reading a book, using methamphetamines."[32] Further, the amount of dopamine released by playing a video game is roughly equivalent to eating a slice of pizza, whereas smoking meth results in a dopamine release ten times more potent.[33]

Przybylski, with regard to the definition supplied to gaming addiction, says, "You could easily take out the word 'gaming' and put in 'sex' or 'food' or 'watching the World Cup.'" In other words, "the gaming disorder definition says nothing about what kinds of games or what features of games might be addicting. So, it's too broad to be helpful."[34]

Przybylski has highlighted that playing video games in moderation has numerous physical and psychological benefits. In an extensive study on this subject, Przybylski found that "there are potential benefits for children who engage in low levels of daily game play (1 to 3 hours a day) and downsides for those who play excessively (more than 3 hours a day)." In other words, from a psychological standpoint, moderation is key when it comes to video games and your children.

*Not addicted does not equal healthy.* The point of all this is not to encourage a hands-off approach regarding your children and gaming. When we look beyond addiction, we find that almost 10 percent of gamers have engaged in problematic play, which negatively impacts their physical or social health. Remember, to qualify as "addicted," gamers must engage in multiple negative behaviors "over a sustained period of three months."[35] In other words, it's quite possible for your children to have a deeply unhealthy level of engagement with games that results in personal harm to themselves and others without being clinically addicted.

As we saw in the last chapter, playing video games in moderation provides numerous benefits. They can help develop problem-solving skills as well as resilience and determination. Video games help us be more productive and improve pattern recognition, concentration, memory, and self-esteem. They can also increase our sense of life satisfaction and provide opportunities for us to bond meaningfully with others. However, these benefits drop dramatically when we play games for extended stretches of three hours or more.[36] Moderation is key. In his study, "Electronic Gaming and Psychological Adjustment," Przybylski found that, "compared with nonplayers, children who spend more than three hours playing video games report higher levels of external and internal problems and lower levels of behavior and life satisfaction."[37]

Even though video game addiction is not as widespread as we might assume, this doesn't mean that irresponsible engagement of games is not. The internet is replete with editorials by concerned parents lamenting their child's relationship with *Fortnite, Minecraft*, or whatever new game is the latest craze. We don't have to wait for our kids to become clinically addicted to encourage them to develop responsible media habits.

Furthermore, we should all educate ourselves on the reward structures of games and how they might affect our brains. Reward structures like loot boxes are common staples in "free-to-play" games that operate similarly to slot machines. Games that eschew loot boxes, like *Fortnite*, often encourage consistent and repeated play through mechanics that prey on children's fears of missing out. Additionally, it has become clear to me over the years that the way we talk about compelling gaming experiences needs to change too.

*Games are partially to blame.* I have been a game critic for over a decade, and I will admit that, for years, I assumed people who play games too much only have themselves to blame. With the handful of times I played games in unhealthy ways, I blamed myself, assuming I was just too invested or too lacking in self-control. While I still believe that the discipline of self-control is the most effective tool we have against unhealthy media habits, I have recently concluded that the way some games are designed should bear some of the blame. I remember the moment I began rethinking this when I read a review written by Russ Pitts of a remake of the classic city builder game *SimCity*. Here is how he described the game:

> From the pleasing sounds of every various button press, to the satisfying way various parts of your city connect, then come to life (then die and come back from the dead), every element of this game has been perfectly and patiently engineered to engender an endorphin rush of accomplishment. . . . In a nutshell, it is the heart and mind of the *SimCity* games of days gone by, but more beautiful, ready to seduce away your hours until you are a rotted husk of the person you used to

> be. If it charged by the hour, you'd sell a kidney. I
> wish I was joking.[38]

Most often when people talk about being addicted to a game, they really mean they just like it a lot and want to play it more—which doesn't qualify as addiction. Pitts does not indicate that he was addicted to *SimCity*. And while Pitts may not have fit the clinical definition for addiction, it's clear there were unhealthy elements of his relationship with the game. However, he didn't cite his own lack of self-control as the culprit. Instead, he says that every element of the game "has been perfectly and patiently engineered to engender an endorphin rush of accomplishment" and to "seduce away your hours until you are a rotted husk of the person you used to be." In fact, later in the review, Pitts said:

> As for how satisfying the experience is as a whole,
> take this example: I missed a meeting. And it
> was my meeting. During the course of one play
> session, I literally became so absorbed in the
> experience that I lost all track of time and played
> through an entire afternoon, oblivious to the fact
> that a meeting I had scheduled approached and
> then passed. When I returned to my workstation
> many, many hours later, I greeted my overflowing
> email in-box and the raft of polite (but concerned)
> inquiries as to my whereabouts with a serene, self-
> possessed calm. As if, whatever troubles the world
> might throw at me would be of little concern next

to the travails I had experienced in West Pittssex
[the name of Pitt's city in *SimCity*].

Then, after a brief, but furiously energized
bout of desk work, I went back to SimCity and did
it all over again.[39]

Pitts wrote this review over eight years ago when there was
very little research about video game addiction, but I have to say
that the way he described *SimCity* was troubling. If a friend of yours
said, "You have to try this brand of vodka—you won't be able to stop
drinking it," you'd be concerned and steer clear of his recommendation. Yet Pitt's description of the *SimCity* remake was intended to
illustrate how great it is and recommend it to others.

Perhaps it's time to come up with other words to describe
what makes some video games so compelling that we want to keep
coming back to them. Perhaps we need to work on this regarding
our favorite TV shows or social media platforms. If we want to set
good examples for our children, we need to be careful about our
habits and how we talk about the aspects we find most engaging.
And if features of some games are designed to take more from us
than they give, maybe we should reconsider whether we want to
play these games or allow our children to play games with such
features.

## Play Better Games

While I personally see a lot of value in playing video games
in moderation, I believe we need to explore the ethics of systems

designed to usurp our time. As a parent, our first goal is helping our children set personal limits, discussing with them the importance of self-control and then developing a strategy for limiting screen time. However, in this day and age, I believe another essential part of our strategy should be helping our children play better games. Simply put, a steady diet of games that employ variable reward systems (things like loot boxes) is not good for children. The psychology employed to create these structures is akin to that which drove the development of slot machines.[40]

Part of why some people find themselves parked at a slot machine in a casino is because the reward they might get is a mystery—when they pull the lever, they could win $5, $0, or a new car. Pediatrician Michael Rich says these reward structures "balance the hope that you are going to make it big with a little bit of frustration, and unlike the slot machine, a sense of skill needed to improve."[41] Some of today's most popular video games reward continued play with random rewards for your character: new costumes, dances, armor, equipment, or weapons. But it isn't just the random nature that keeps gamers playing; it's the randomness tied with the possibility of getting something rare and unique.

Many games today also have their own economies which encourage continued play. One of the most famous examples of this is the widely popular online battle royale game *Fortnite*. At the height of its popularity in the fall of 2018, hardly a day went by without an editorial or video being published by a concerned parent lamenting their children's obsession with *Fortnite*. Depending on who you talk to, *Fortnite* is either a colorful game that promotes creative problem-solving and team-building or something more akin to drug addiction. Though *Fortnite* is a third-person shooter, what I find troubling about *Fortnite* is not its cartoon violence but the way it rewards players through its in-game store.

*Fortnite* trains players to maintain a steady diet of the game to keep earning "V-bucks" to spend on skins (new looks or costumes) and emotes (dances or taunts your character can do). Dozens of other games operate similarly, but *Fortnite* is simply the most popular game to employ these compulsion-driven reward systems.[42] *Fortnite*, however, appeals to a slightly younger demographic than the average shooter due to its colorful aesthetic and less visually graphic violence. Younger kids in large numbers are playing this game and being introduced to its reward systems. Even though the game has been around since 2017, it's likely that your preteen still won't shut up about it. Game critic Peter Farquhar recently wrote an editorial for Business Insider on this subject and concluded: "There are literally hundreds of thousands of video games for your kids to play that don't cause problems in households. *Fortnite* isn't one of them."[43]

Zach Carpenter, writing for Love Thy Nerd, explains how the game's economy works:

> *Fortnite Battle Royale* is free to download and play, but it makes money through microtransactions— players can purchase things like outfits (known as "skins") and dances. Epic, the publisher of *Fortnite,* creates the illusion of scarcity of demand because their store only has those skins for a day or two. Then they are gone (they will come back

eventually . . . and usually for less . . . you just have
to wait a long time).[44]

The combination of *Fortnite's* popularity, the limited avail-
ability of the items in its store, and the limited amount of V-bucks
players can earn by merely playing the game (rather than spending
real money) is a recipe for young people to beg their parents for
money and/or more game time. *Fortnite,* however, is far from the
only game adopting these kinds of borderline exploitative reward
systems. You've probably heard your kids talk about "free-to-play"
games. While these games are free to download, they make money
through in-game purchases (often referred to as "microtransactions") or advertisements. These types of games are notorious for
employing reward structures that take advantage of children's lack
of self-control similar to games like *Fortnite.*[45]

It is unfortunate that *Fortnite* and many other free-to-play
games are causing so many parents to hate video games because
Farquhar is right—there are "hundreds of thousands of video
games" that don't cause problems in the home. And the reason these
other games don't cause problems is because they provide healthier
rewards that don't encourage compulsive behavior. In fact, these
games provide kids and parents with intrinsic rewards that are far
more valuable than extrinsic rewards like skins or emotes. There
are games where the reward is the play experience itself or the satisfaction of solving a problem, overcoming an obstacle, or winning a
competition that requires teamwork. There are games you can play
with your kids that help them build healthier relationships—both
with technology and with you. In fact, we compiled a list of eight

such games at Love Thy Nerd to help you get started.[46] I would also recommend checking out the database of video games at Taming Gaming, which actually has a feature that allows you to exclude games with loot boxes when you search the database.[47] Taming Gaming also provides curated lists with great recommendations for family-friendly games based on the age of your children.[48]

As we have seen, many video games, when played in moderation or played socially, can have a positive impact on our development, our brains, and our real-world relationships. God has so shaped the human body that everything we do impacts our brains. It's crucial that we steward them well. Finally, it's also important to remember the mission God has given us in this world to make disciples. Video games are played by 214 million Americans.[49] These are people, made in the image of God, that we might reach with ministry if we'd make an honest effort to understand them and their hobby of choice.

Having tackled two of the most troubling aspects about video games, I would be remiss not to mention another area where the medium has a lot of growing to do: how video games depict women.

## Misogyny and Sexual Content

In January 2013, *Dead Island: Riptide* publisher Deep Silver announced that fans of the soon-to-be released game could get a statue of a busty, bloody, bikini-clad female torso with its arms and head severed along with the special edition of the game.

So there you have it—the two Achilles' heels of the gaming industry right there in one limited-edition package: glorified, horrific violence, and objectified, oversexualized women epitomized in this one piece of kitsch. Most people saw this bloodied torso for what it was: a shocking display of sexualized violence the likes of which most of the world would prefer never to see.

Understandably, outrage ensued. And yet someone signed off on this idea to the point that it went to print after likely passing the desks of more than one person. Presumably, the bloody, bikini-clad torso made it past a brainstorming team, concept artists, and proofreaders, none of whom thought to pump the brakes on the idea before it was lampooned by the media. In fact, several of these sexualized torsos made it into the homes of people who purchased the special edition. This tells us that there was a group of people—as determined by a marketing team at a huge video game publisher—who looked at this thing and thought it was cool.

### *Misogyny*

That was nearly a decade ago, but it illustrates the checkered past of video games when it comes to the representation of women. Take a glance at the best-selling video games and the latest video game commercials at any given moment, and you would assume that video games are predominantly played by men. Market research, however, paints a much less drastic disparity. For the last decade, women have made up at least 40 percent of all gamers and as much as 46 percent as recently as 2019.[50] And still there are few female lead characters in the most successful game franchises, and those games that do feature female leads tend to depict them in overly sexualized ways.

The *Grand Theft Auto* (GTA) series is one of the most glaring examples. At the time of its release, Carolyn Petit was an editor for one of the largest video game sites, Gamespot, and she reviewed GTA V. In her review, she called the game "profoundly misogynic":

> GTA V has little room for women except to por-
> tray them as strippers, prostitutes, long-suffering
> wives, humorless girlfriends and goofy, new-age
> feminists we're meant to laugh at.
>
> Characters constantly spout lines that glorify
> male sexuality while demeaning women, and the
> billboards and radio stations of the world rein-
> force this misogyny, with ads that equate man-
> hood with sleek sports cars while encouraging
> women to purchase a fragrance that will make
> them "smell like a bitch." Yes, these are exaggera-
> tions of misogynistic undercurrents in our own
> society, but not satirical ones. With nothing in the
> narrative to underscore how insane and wrong
> this is, all the game does is reinforce and celebrate
> sexism.[51]

Petit's review, aside from these criticisms about the game's depiction of women, was largely complimentary of GTA V. (She said the game "has one of the most beautiful, lively, diverse and stimu-lating worlds ever seen."[52]) Her review was met with more than twenty-two thousand comments; however, the majority took issue with her criticism. Commenters, most of whom were male, called

Petit names and dismissed her as a "feminist." They accosted her for giving the game a lower score than most other outlets (an impressive 9 out of 10) and accused her of devaluing games as an art form. Many male gamers claimed that GTA V's portrayal of women was satirical and intended to expose unchecked sexism in America. The problem with this theory is that satire typically provides a foil, but no positive portrayals of women existed in GTA V to drive home the contrast amid the excess. This essentially left male gamers to revel in their prejudice. While a large portion of video game players are female, the majority of GTA fans are male, and the response to Petit's review illustrates why it might be unwise to present a young male audience with so much unchecked misogyny.

The problem with portrayals of women that diminish and sexualize them is that they can cultivate sexist attitudes and behaviors. Dr. Rachel Kowert, reflecting on research on this subject, says, "Constant and prolonged exposure to the underrepresentation of women in video games is thought to cultivate sexist thoughts, attitudes, and behaviors among the mostly male video game players."[53] If young people regularly play video games with unflattering and stereotypical portrayals of women, the interactive space of a video game can become a highly influential method of teaching prejudice against women, whether intentional or not.[54] This concern grows with teenage players, as they are at greater risk for influence via media.[55]

### Toxicity

Problematic attitudes are not merely represented in popular video games themselves but also in the behavior of their players online. Nearly two thirds of women who play games online report being recipients of sexist or misogynistic behavior from other players.[56] A 2013 study found that "in game chatter using a female voice earned Xbox Live players three times as much verbal abuse as using a male voice."[57] And while female players are at greater risk than their male counterparts, anyone who plays games online regularly is likely to experience bullying or verbal abuse or even targeted harassment. In fact, a recent survey of adult gamers aged eighteen to forty-five found that 74 percent say they have experienced some form of harassment while playing online games, and 65 percent reported experiencing "severe harassment," such as physical threats, sustained harassment, and stalking.[58]

So if you let your children play games online, the question is not *if* they'll be harassed so much as *when*. And while most of the harassment they will face is primarily verbal, there are predators that pose as children to lure them into inappropriate communication through online gaming.[59] And of course, various social media apps, like Kik Messenger, are often even more problematic in this regard. So it is not just online gaming that you should be concerned about. In other words, a hands-off approach regarding your children's online activities is not a risk you should take. This doesn't mean that online games should be completely avoided. As I have stated previously, there are still many benefits to online games like friendship and teamwork. Thankfully, there are ways you can make your children's online gaming experiences safer by limiting and monitoring who they can and can't interact with online. In fact, the tools for protecting children most gaming platforms provide are far more robust and helpful than what is available on most social media platforms. We will touch on this in the next chapter, but for now, I simply want to make you aware of these dangers.

## *Sexual Content*

In 2004, *Grand Theft Auto: San Andreas* made headlines due to a secret, sexually explicit mod (modification) discovered by players. It was called "Hot Coffee." In the scene, the game's lead character has sexual intercourse with an in-game girlfriend of a player's choosing. While the scene was excluded from the published version of the game, players discovered assets for the scene and modified the game to make it accessible. It wasn't long before this secret scene was all anyone was talking about regarding *GTA: San Andreas*. This was a major moment in video game history because, up to this point, mainstream video games were largely devoid of nudity. Following criticism from lawmakers and the public, *GTA: San Andreas* was given an AO (adults only) rating in the U.S. by the Entertainment Software Rating Board (ESRB). The game was even withdrawn from sale altogether in Australia until the assets for the scene were removed completely. Today, the "Hot Coffee" controversy seems like a distant memory. Games like *The Witcher* series, *Cyberpunk 2077*, the *God of War* series, and *Rust* all contain full-frontal nudity. Thankfully, nudity is always noted in the ESRB's rating of these games, and knowing what kind of content is in games is easier today than ever before. Still, you should know that explicit sexual content is no longer taboo or even particularly rare in the world of electronic gaming.

Kowert says, "Researchers have found that male players who are exposed to stereotypical representations of women in video games report to being more tolerant of sexual harassment. . . . However, when following the same players over time, no evidence has been found to indicate that sexist beliefs become cultivated over time due to video game play alone."[60] When it comes to helping your children respect and honor other people, how characters are depicted matters, but video games are just one of many influencers.

These findings tell us that it's not enough to merely monitor the kinds of games your children play; you also need to talk to them about what they are already playing. Conversely, if you are going to withhold certain games from them due to their content, you need to be prepared to explain why. Your children need to understand that your concern is that they see themselves and their neighbors accurately—as people made in the image of a good God with inherent dignity and worthy of respect. When you see characters in the games they play or the shows they watch behaving immaturely or stereotypically, ask them what they think about that. We can't trust the surrounding culture to help our children develop a more robust and nuanced understanding of their worth and identity. Objectifying and disempowering portrayals of women are not unique to video games. Even if you were to outlaw video games in your home, you'd still need to discuss these things with your children in contrast to what is often displayed on social media, on television, in comics, in film, and on billboards.

The landscape of representation in video games, as in many other forms of media, is rapidly changing along with our culture. In reviewing the announcements of major video game publishers at 2020's E3 (Electronic Entertainment Expo) conference, the premier video game trade show of the year, female lead characters were featured in 18 percent of games in the show. That's an increase from an average of 5 percent over the last decade.[61] Games are moving toward a more inclusive and healthier depiction of women, but it's important to be aware of both video games' checkered past regarding representation as well as the kind of content your children are likely to come across if you don't provide them with boundaries (which is the focus on the next chapter).

Hopefully by now, you are picking up on a key theme in this book: the importance of conversation. If you want to see your children flourish, your strategy must go deeper than a set of rules. Simply put, you need to make a regular habit of conversing with your children about the games they play or want to play. Don't preach at them, but really talk to them: ask questions and express genuine interest and curiosity in their perspective. This will foster an environment in which you can speak clearly and redemptively about crucial subjects such as sex, violence, and addiction. It will also foster an environment in which your children are far more likely to listen and grow.

This chapter has likely been both eye-opening and alarming. Eye-opening because we've made an effort to get to the bottom of the most troubling aspects of video games and their potential impact on our children, and alarming because video games are— like everything else in God's good world—broken. They have the potential to boost our creativity, community, and happiness, but they also can be abused and misused and even sometimes contain content that objectifies and demeans people made in God's image.

So in the next chapter, I hope to help you formulate a plan that will work for you and your family to help you get the best out of what video games have to offer while avoiding the worst.

# Games Are Complicated

Remember when I said video games could be played for the glory of God? If your child's obsession with video games is a constant battle in your home, you might have been tempted to put the book down right then and there. But if you are still reading, chances are you haven't been winning the video game battle with your kids. You may even be seriously considering raising the white flag. When you allow your children to play video games, the time limits you set never satisfy your children. And once the games are off, they never seem interested in doing anything else. It can almost feel like your children are now punishing you with their bad attitudes for not allowing them to play more. If you aren't careful, repeated behavior like this from your children can cause you to not only despise video games but even resent your children. Remember that your primary job as a parent is to love your children.

But listen, I get it. Navigating this seemingly endless cycle of limiting your children's game time, dealing with their bad attitudes, and giving in and letting them have more screen time—only to later regret that decision—is exhausting. And finding the right balance of how much screen time to allow your kids, learning how to protect them online, and knowing what kinds of games they should and shouldn't play can feel complicated and overwhelming. Add to this the fact that the world of video games is growing and changing at an incredibly rapid rate, and the world of video games can start to feel impossibly complex.

Navigating the world of video games isn't as difficult as you might think. So the goal of this chapter is to help you develop a strategy and equip you to help your children engage games responsibly and in a Christlike manner.

## Start with Love

We are about to discuss many ideas and strategies you can employ to protect and guide your children, but every single strategy will backfire if you lose sight of the ultimate goal of parenting: to love your children.

Loving your children well requires making an intentional effort to know them and develop a close personal relationship with them. Your goal in parenting your children should never be to manipulate their behavior to come in line with your vision for them. Too often we fall into the trap of asking ourselves: "How can I get my children to do what I want?" Your children may never do what you want or submit to your vision for their lives. Pushing so hard for them to fall into step may very well be pushing them further away. We may even reach out to others for help in ways that aren't healthy by pleading, "Please help me fix my children!" Your children don't need fixing. Your child's interest in video games doesn't make them foolish or lazy or immature. So let go of the labels and focus on loving the children God has given you. Rather than seeking to get our children to do what we want, we need to consider how we can better relate to and grow in relationship with our children.

In my experience, just bringing up the subject of video games makes a lot of parents angry. I get why video games can be triggering, given they are the source of so much tension and conflict in your home. Trust me, my wife and I have been there. We get it. However, we must remember what Paul told the church at Ephesus: "Don't stir up anger in your children, but bring them up in the training and instruction of the Lord" (Eph. 6:4). If your children can't talk about video games without you getting angry, your most crucial action after reading this chapter is to sincerely apologize to them. Your children are not responsible for your anger or bad attitude toward them and their interest in video games. No matter how frustrating your children's behavior is, they are not responsible for your feelings and actions. You are. What your children need to know above all is that you care about them.

So before we tap into some strategies for guiding your children, now is the time for you to determine to know and love thy gamer. I would even suggest taking a moment to jot down a prayer to God, asking Him to help you fight the temptation of bitterness toward your children. Ask Him to replace any resentment with love and irritation at your children's gaming habits with curiosity about who they are and what holds their interest.

All parents need to face a harsh reality that there is a good chance that playing video games will be the most interesting thing their children do on a given day. When they go to school, band practice, or church, they won't be saving the world from alien invasion or building a magnificent seaside castle like they do in *Halo* or *Minecraft*. The potential of video games to whisk us off to new worlds and empower us to accomplish great feats is a big part of what makes them special. Video games are part of God's good creation, but like all good things, they can be exploited, misused, and abused. So this chapter is full of tips to help you navigate gaming more effectively. I will help you develop strategies for limiting game time, staying connected to your children, protecting your children online, and monitoring what your children are playing.

While parenting is more akin to a marathon than a sprint, my prayer is that this chapter feels like a cheat code that makes navigating video games a bit easier. If you're not sure what a cheat code is, they are little codes or sequences that allow you to unlock things like access to hidden levels, endless amounts of money, or even unlimited lives. My goal is to help you unlock ways to help your children navigate the world of video games in a Christlike manner so that they might play them in ways that lead to their flourishing rather than their detriment.

## Help Your Children Diversify Their Free Time

Childhood, particularly early adolescence, is an excellent time to introduce your children to a diversity of interests and hobbies. You don't have to ask my children if they want to play video games—the answer is always yes. If we ask them if they want to go hiking, however, their responses have been mixed. Occasionally, one or more of my children are really opposed to the idea of hiking. Nevertheless, we make them go. We believe it is vital to their mental, emotional, and spiritual well-being to enjoy creation and exercise. We have found that, even when we force them, they almost always have a really good time on our family hikes. In other words, just because your children act like video games are the only things that bring them joy, that's not actually true.

All children need encouragement from their parents or caregivers to try new activities and hobbies. They need your support to become more resilient and confident. My children have requested to quit just about every extracurricular activity they have participated in at one point or another, even the ones they love the most. Your children need you to say no when they ask to quit after the first soccer game or dance class. They also need you to listen when they share how embarrassed they were when their coach or teacher yelled at them at practice in front of everyone. Parenting well requires challenging your kids to persevere when things go wrong, while also studying and listening to their unique personalities, giftings, and interests. Your goal is to respect and honor the unique way God has shaped them.

If you insist on introducing your children to new hobbies and activities, they are almost certain to find things they enjoy, whether that's playing an instrument, dancing, drama, hiking, cycling, skating, playing board games, or something else. We should also note that kids learn to enjoy different activities at different ages. As someone who has coached soccer for over a decade, I can't tell you how many times I have seen young players cry when put in a game one season only to cry the next season when they must come off the field. Just because a particular activity doesn't seem to gel with them one year, doesn't mean they won't love it later when you encourage them to try again.

You will also likely come to the point where you may have to admit that certain hobbies you've introduced just aren't their thing. While writing this, I'm trying to decide whether to insist on taking my daughters on more mountain bike rides or if it's time for me to come to terms with their lack of interest in my personal favorite sport. There isn't any right or wrong answer. On the one hand, I know that mountain biking is good for young people's confidence and physical well-being. I also know that mountain biking has been a tremendous source of social connection for me as I have developed strong, meaningful friendships through the sport. If my girls were to take a strong liking to mountain biking, it would give us a hobby we could enjoy together for a long time. On the other hand, I can't make my kids enjoy the activities I enjoy. God calls me to love the children He has given me, not the children I want them to be. So my advice is to have them try lots of new activities, but once they have given a new activity a fair chance, don't force them to keep at it if it's clearly not their thing.

We don't let our kids quit midway through the soccer season. And if we signed on for the recital, our kids are going to stay in dance until that's complete. However, we make a point to listen to our children and give them a real say in what hobbies they pursue and even what activities we do together as a family.

Lately, my eldest daughter only seems interested in playing *Roblox* on the iPad. The only other thing she gets as excited about is playing with her best friend who lives down the street from us. We are not, however, letting her choose *Roblox* over other activities we know might be good for her. This means we are forcing her to stick with dance. We have also signed her up for fall soccer, but these are activities she has also agreed to. She also said she'd enjoy playing soccer more if I were her coach. (Guess who's coaching soccer in the fall.)

These efforts are examples of how my wife and I, as parents, try to meet our eldest daughter where she is. We know she needs other activities and experiences in her life besides *Roblox*. Deep down, I think she knows it too. So loving her well, for us, means not only limiting her time on the iPad but also working with her on incorporating other activities into her routine while still giving her a legitimate voice in these decisions. If you will give your kids a voice in the activities they pursue, they will be more likely to invest in them on a higher level, and they'll be less likely to complain or ask to quit.

## Lower the Stakes

Video games have been around long enough that I have dozens of friends who worried that their children were addicted to video games at one point. However, the children of these parents have grown up and are responsible, balanced, and productive young adults. This is also true of me. I have never been close to clinically addicted, but there were times in middle school and high school when video games were all I really wanted to do. There were times my parents worried about me, but I got over that. I learned new habits and managed to graduate near the top of my class in both college and seminary before going on to live a productive, balanced, happy life. This isn't to say that your children's unhealthy fixation on video games isn't an important problem to address now but, rather, to encourage you not to place undue pressure on yourself to fix your child before it's too late. It isn't too late, and, remember, your children don't need fixing. They need your love, protection, guidance, and support.

One of the common temptations to parenthood is to think that one small mistake, like buying your kids a Nintendo or giving them too much screen time, is going to ruin them. This is called catastrophizing—we think one bad decision could ruin our lives or the lives of our children. This kind of thinking is destructive because it creates a false sense of reality. When you do this, you are making your children's situation out to be way worse than it really is, and, as a result, you contribute more stress and frustration to the relationship.

The decisions you make about your children and video games are not going to make or break them. And honestly, if you keep thinking like that, you are contributing to conversations about video games ending in tears and screams. When it comes to rules regarding video games and screen time, you will make mistakes. There are going to be days when you throw your hands up and let them play video games all day. This doesn't make you a failure as a parent. Tomorrow is a new day for you and your children. No matter how poorly you feel like you've handled video games in your home, it's not too late for your kids. Their current obsession with *Fortnite* or *Minecraft* or *Call of Duty* is unlikely to persist forever, nor is it likely to lead them on a path toward utter failure or abject poverty.

Now that we have appropriately lowered the stakes on the video game battle, let's talk about your most immediate need when it comes to helping your children navigate the world of video games: limiting their screen time.

## Screen Time

Before we discuss some strategies for handling screen time in your family, it's important to try to understand its appeal and its impact on our children as well as what children today are doing most often on screens.

Teenagers are spending more time in front of screens than ever before, but not as much of that time is spent gaming as the latest video game addiction headlines might make you think. One Hope's recent study on Global Youth Culture found that "teens are online all the time. Not literally, but close to it. Teens in the U.S. are spending an average of 7 hours and 35 minutes online daily."[1] A recent study by Common Sense Media also revealed a substantial disparity in screen use by kids from high- and low-income families, with children from lower-income families using screens an hour and fifty minutes more per day than those from higher-income families.[2] Given your child's seeming obsession with video games, you'll be surprised to learn that most of those seven and a half hours are not devoted to gaming. In fact, teens spend less time playing games online than they do chatting, using social media, and watching videos.

Our children have more distractions at their fingertips than ever before. There is YouTube, Twitch, TikTok, Twitter, Snapchat,

Netflix, and Instagram. By the time this book is published, there will probably be new apps, social media platforms, and devices soaking up (or threatening to soak up) more and more of your kids' time and attention. As we have seen, video games are much less passive than most of the other things your children do on screens. Yes, social media is interactive, but if we are honest, most of us would admit that the vast majority of the time we spend on social media is not spent actively posting and commenting but passively scrolling.

More important, most of the social media apps are actively studying (or spying on) our likes and interests in order to advertise new products to us.[3] To be frank, I would rather have my kids playing video games than a lot of other things they might be doing on screens. When kids play video games, they are actively using their brains to solve problems, recognize patterns, and communicate with other players. In other words, not all screen time is created equal, nor does all screen time have the same impact on children.

Pediatrician Michael Rich, who has been helping parents navigate screen time with their children for years, says:

> We have to be flexible enough to evolve with the technology but choose how to use it right. Fire was a great discovery to cook our food, but we had to learn it could hurt and kill as well. . . .
>
> We don't want to be in a moral panic because kids are staring at smartphones. We need to be asking, what's happening when they're staring at their smartphone in terms of their cognitive,

social, and emotional development? As with most things, it will probably be a mix of positive and negative. Going forward with our eyes open, how can we enhance the positive and mitigate the negative?[4]

I would add spiritual formation to Rich's list. I also want to consider how my kids' game time relates to their worldview, their relationships with others, their sense of purpose, and their relationship with God. I believe how our children play games can benefit or hinder their spiritual well-being. One of the primary ways we do this is by helping our children set limits for their time on screens.

So this brings up the ultimate question about screen time: How much is too much?

## How Much Is Too Much?

I wish I could give you a magic number that's perfect for every child of every age and family situation, but the reality is that every child is unique, and what works for some may not work for others. What I can tell you is that all children need limits—their brains are not yet fully developed and lack the self-control necessary to know when screen time is becoming detrimental. Reviewing research on children and screen time, both the American Academy of Pediatricians (AAP) and the World Health Organization (WHO) have set forth recommended guidelines for children's screen time.

The AAP recommends:[5]

- No screen time at all for children until eighteen to twenty-four months, except for video chatting.
- Kids two to five years old should get an hour or less of screen time per day.
- Grade-schoolers/teens: Don't let media displace other important activities such as quality sleep, regular exercise, family meals, and "unplugged" downtime.
- Creating a Family Media Use Plan for older kids, an online resource which helps parents and children negotiate rules and limits regarding screen time.[6]
- Setting media-free times and limiting exposure to screens one to two hours before bedtime.
- Co-viewing media and discussing it, when possible, to enhance learning.[7]

The WHO recommends:[8]

- Infants (less than one year of age): Screen time is not recommended.
- No screen time for one-year-olds.
- No more than an hour a day for two-year-olds, with less time preferred.
- No more than one hour a day for three- to four-year-olds.

Both organizations highlight various negative consequences for too much screen time for young children. The WHO warns against the dangers of a sedentary lifestyle, which has been identified as a risk factor in global mortality. They also claim that too much screen time can have a negative impact on children's communication, decision-making, and problem-solving skills.

The AAP's and WHO's recommendations and conclusions regarding screen time are based on research that does not differentiate between different types of screen use. For instance, talking to Grandma on FaceTime is not the same as watching Netflix—the former is healthier for our brains than the latter. And many video games are likely engaging children's brains on a higher level than FaceTime or Netflix. Don't forget everything we unpacked in the last chapter about how video games, in moderation, can be good for kids. As we read the AAP's and WHO's recommendations, we should also remember that studying the long-term impact of screen time on children is very difficult. We live in a highly connected world, so it is nearly impossible to observe a large sample size of children over long periods of time who have little to no exposure to screens in order to observe their developmental differences from those who are regularly on screens. Imagine how most parents would react if asked to allow their children to participate in a study where their children would be in front of screens for six or more hours a day.

Most families today are not following the WHO or AAP guidelines. We have already seen that teens are spending more than an average of seven hours a day online. Families of younger children are also not following the AAP and WHO guidelines. A recently published study found that from 1997 to 2014, screen time for children aged two and under more than doubled from 1 hour and 19 minutes to 3 hours and 3 minutes.[9] And that was 2014—we know that screen use increased during the COVID-19 pandemic. For example, a survey during the pandemic showed that nearly seven out of ten parents said that their children spent more time on screens during the pandemic, and 63 percent of parents lowered their standards for what they deem appropriate screen time for their children.[10]

And let's be honest, you probably don't strictly abide by the WHO's or the AAP's guidelines either. Sometimes you do. There have probably been times when you felt like you had a handle on screen time and were enforcing appropriate limits that were keeping your kids happy and healthy. There were likely other times when you just needed to get something done so you let your kids watch a movie or five episodes of *Paw Patrol* or play who knows how many hours of *Minecraft*. You're reading this book because you know these decisions were mistakes. You are not alone. My wife and I have made plenty of screen-time mistakes with our children as well, but it doesn't help to dwell on these past failures. Guilt is a terrible motivator. Instead, forgive yourself for these missteps, and take a positive step forward this week. Set aside some time to jot down your ideal screen-time policies and procedures for you and your family. If you are married, spend some time this week discussing a screen-time plan with your partner. If you are a single parent, consider discussing a possible screen-time plan with a trusted friend. Discussing this with a trusted friend will help you develop a more effective plan and will also help you feel less alone as a parent or caregiver.

### Screen-Time Tips

I can't give you a perfect time limit based on the age of your children, but I can give you some tips for how to develop rules for your family as well as some potential strategies for handling screen time at home. Let's start with the tips, then we will get into the strategies. Kendra Adachi, the "Lazy Genius," says whatever rules you make should be clear, collaborative, and written down.[11]

### Clear

Your children need to be crystal clear on when they can and can't play video games. They also need to be crystal clear on what will happen if they break these rules. If there are certain days or types of days that have different rules or limits (i.e., less screen time on school days than on weekends), this needs to be clearly but concisely communicated to your children. If you can't explain your house rules regarding screens to your kids in less than a minute, you can be sure your children are going to either forget important details, break rules unintentionally, or feign ignorance when caught breaking them. If your rules are too complex, you won't know if they are telling the truth when they break them or be entirely sure whether your child's behavior is in step with the rules. For example, it's fine to have different rules for weekends than weekdays, but if every day of the week has a different set of rules, you can be sure your children will get mixed up, and you probably will too.

The point of all family rules should be to promote your children's flourishing. Guidelines should be designed to set them up for success. Overly complicated rules set your children up for failure and set you up for frustration. Drawing up clear rules and guidelines might seem obvious, but if you don't prioritize clarity, you'll be surprised by how quickly your house rules become a source of frustration.

## Collaborative

One of the most demoralizing aspects of setting screen limits is the tension between you and your children that comes with them. You may have even plotted new screen-time guidelines, but you are avoiding enforcing the new rules because you dread the argument and bad attitudes that are sure to follow. One of the simplest ways to avoid this is to involve your children. If your children feel like they have a genuine voice in whatever policies and procedures you come up with, they will respect those policies more and will be less likely to deem them unjust. After all, they helped develop the policy. I know what you might be thinking: *If I let my children have a voice in their screen limits, they are going to ask for unlimited screen time or something unreasonable like eight hours a day.* I would encourage you not to sell your children short. They likely know unlimited screen time isn't healthy and might surprise you with some reasonable ideas that you could work with. I would recommend against asking them: "How much screen time do you think you should get?" and, instead, ask something like: "If you were a parent, what rules would you set for your children with regard to screen time?"

More than just setting rules to protect your children, you need to do the hard but invaluable work of explaining why these rules exist. Your children need to feel loved and protected. Sharing why you set the rules you set is crucial to fulfilling those roles as their parent. Asking them to consider what they would do in your shoes does two things: it allows them to share their perspective, and it provides an opportunity for you to share your heart.

Before you ask your children what they would do in your shoes, you need to have an idea in your mind of what kinds of screen-time rules and limits you'd like to set. If you are married, involve your spouse in determining a plan so that when you discuss screen time with your children, you are both prepared to work toward the policies you'd like to set. Please do not misunderstand me; I am not at all suggesting that you let your children dictate their own screen time. I am, however, suggesting that you set their screen-time limits in the context of a real, meaningful discussion where you make a genuine effort to listen to them. If your children insist that if they were parents, they would give their children unlimited screen time, keep asking follow-up questions: "Why? What do you think might happen to your children if they did not have any screen-time limits? Why do you think I try to limit your screen time?"

It is certainly possible to lay down the law on gaming and screen time. You are the parent, so if you don't want to invite your children to collaborate with you on the rules, you certainly don't have to. However, your goal in these discussions is not to win the argument on screen time but to demonstrate care for your children. The constant battle over screen time can put you on edge. After all, every parent wants to be respected by their children. We, however, should remind ourselves that our primary goal is not to be respected by our children but to love them. When we keep this at the forefront, we won't be content with merely compliant children, and we won't take it personally when our children disobey.

I am reminded of how Jesus taught on the law in the Sermon on the Mount. His issue was not with the law itself but with how it had been interpreted. He said, "You have heard that it was said to our ancestors, 'Do not murder'. . . . But I tell you, everyone who is angry with his brother or sister will be subject to judgment" (Matt. 5:21–22a). In other words, Jesus wasn't content with just laying down the law. He was genuinely concerned that people understood God's heart behind the law, which ultimately leads to human flourishing.

Equally important to setting boundaries around screen time is helping your children see the reasoning behind those boundaries. When your children see that the limits you set are ultimately rooted in love, they will be more likely not only to respect your rules but flourish under them.

Your children may never get on the same page with you about screen time, and, despite your best efforts, they may never understand why you insist on limiting screen time. Your job as a parent is not to change your children's hearts and minds. At some points in parenting, you have to be content with setting the best boundaries you can, communicating the intent behind them, and entrusting the hearts of your children to the Lord.

### Written

Writing your rules and guidelines down is as much for you as it is for your children. It's a way of formalizing your plan and ensuring that it is clear. This process of writing your rules down makes them clear for everyone involved—you, your children, your spouse (if you have one), and anyone who might watch your children. If you want to enforce your screen-time rules when your children are being watched by grandparents or a babysitter, your rules must be clear and written down. If your rules are not simple enough to write down, then they are not simple enough for your children to follow or anyone but you to enforce. Prior to your family meeting with your children, write down your ideal rules. Review them with your spouse or a sympathetic friend. The writing process will help you identify if your boundaries are clear enough for your children to understand and for you to enforce.

## *Set a Good Example*

There is a good chance you or your spouse are gamers. You may not think of yourself this way, but if you take out your phone to play *Fantasy Football*, *Words with Friends*, *Candy Crush Saga*, *Wordle*, or *Fallout Shelter*, you are a gamer. And even if you are not a gamer, you almost certainly have a smartphone, and your children will notice if you check it at every dull moment. They won't differentiate what you are doing from their interest in video games because your children will struggle to respect the boundaries you set for them if they see you or your partner operate with little to no boundaries regarding screens.

Half of all kids and three-quarters of parents feel the other is distracted when talking to each other.[12] It doesn't matter if you are reading the Bible on your phone or responding to an important work email. Don't let your phone distract you from being attentive and engaged with your children. You might also consider setting up some screen-free zones in your home (the dinner table is a good one) and maybe some screen-free hours of the day as well. This is as much or more for you as it is for your children.

Your children don't need a parent who never fails to set limits and self-regulate their own screen time. They need to see a parent who is trying. Don't expect that you will set a perfect example for your children because you will fail. If you are often tempted to mindlessly scroll through Facebook, watch video after video on YouTube, or play video games for hours on end, you shouldn't completely hide such struggles from your children. Admit your own weaknesses and failures to your children. When your children see you setting a poor example with your screen time, they are likely to call you out. If this happens, don't be defensive. If your children see you put up your phone when they call you out, they will see a parent who is making an effort to be present and to live by your own guidelines. Your vulnerability and honesty will invite the same from your children. Furthermore, you will not be able to hide your own struggles and failures from your children forever. The better tactic is to admit the areas where you are weak and the areas where you strive to improve. If you'll be appropriately honest with your children about these things, they will see someone coming alongside them to develop healthy habits rather than someone who merely wants to dictate their behavior or, worse—a hypocrite.

### *Compare Notes, Not Children*

There are countless home rules when it comes to video games and screen time. Every family is unique and has different values, needs, and differently wired children. It's helpful to discuss what you are doing regarding screen time with trusted friends who share your values. Think of this as comparing notes: What is working or not working for your friends who are parents? When you have these conversations, remember that your family is unique (so don't feel pressured to adopt anyone else's policies), but these conversations can give you insight into what policies you might want to implement in your home.

It is crucial, however, that you compare notes, not children. You probably have friends who seem to have the video game battle handled; their kids seem to comply with whatever screen-time limits they set without complaint. You'll have other friends who brag about how little their children even want to watch TV or play video games. This does not mean such people are better parents or that you have failed your kids. Do what is best for your children in the context of your home, your desires, your needs, and your uniquely wired children. Think of these conversations as opportunities to refine how you handle screen time with your kids, but do not let what others are doing fill your heart with anxiety or guilt.

Be careful how you talk about your screen-time policies with other parents. Most parents are on high alert when it comes to screen time. Be careful not to make other parents feel inferior if they've got less of a handle on screen time than you do. It's more likely that you feel like you have a lot of work to do on the screen-time front. Eventually, however, you'll get to a place where you are proud of the progress you have made navigating this space with your children. While that's a wonderful place to be, you'll want to be extra careful not to make other parents feel inferior for being in a different stage. Parent shaming doesn't help us or others, so be careful not to offer unsolicited advice. Be sympathetic and offer suggestions when asked. Strive to be a good friend.

### Make Screen Time Work for You

If you are thinking about screen time primarily in terms of what is best for your children, you are only thinking about half of the equation. You need to consider yourself—your needs, desires, and responsibilities. Your children's screen-time rules need not only work for your children but for you as well.

For many parents, particularly single parents and parents of children under the age of ten, screen time might be one of the few times during the day when you get a break or are free to get things done around the house without interruption. While I believe it can be really beneficial to play video games with your children, you may need to use their screen time for some self-care or to get things done around the house without interruption. Decide what you need to do during their screen time and stick to it. If you don't have a plan for how you want to spend your time while they are getting their screen time, there is a good chance you'll regret your decision and end up giving in to your children's pleas for more. Part of why some parents end up regretting the amount of time their children spend on screens is because they keep giving in when their children beg for one more game or one more episode.

### Preview the Day

Most children do well when what's expected of them is clear. It can be helpful to go over what's in store for the day each morning at breakfast or, if mornings are hectic, each night at dinner or just before bedtime. These are opportunities to remind them of what the day holds in terms of screen time: "Remember, tomorrow is a school day, so you'll get thirty minutes of screen time after you finish your homework," or "Tomorrow is Saturday and we are going camping, so you'll get your screen time in the car on the way to the state park but no screen time while we are camping." Giving your children a heads-up about what each day brings sets them up for success and lessens the likelihood of an argument.

### Don't Make Screen-Time Changes When You Are Frustrated

Because most parents are heavily invested in screen time, we swing between trying to eliminate it from the lives of our children altogether to giving them all the screen time they want because we are exhausted. Knowing this tells us two things: you will inevitably decide how you want to make changes to your house screen-time rules, and you are most likely to make these changes reactively rather than proactively. In other words, the moment you are most likely to make changes to screen-time rules is the moment when your children's behavior is irritating you the most. This is the worst time to make changes because both you and your children are on edge. Remember your goal as a parent is not to fix your children but to love them. When you are deeply frustrated with their screen-time use, fight the temptation to launch into stringent new policies. Give yourself some time to think about it or talk it over with a trusted friend or your spouse. It might feel really good, cathartic even, to foist a screen-time ban on your child when he is throwing a tantrum about having to turn off his favorite show. Know yourself well enough to push pause on making important parenting decisions when your nerves are shot and your energy tank is low.

Just as you are on high alert about video games and screen time, your children are on high alert, too, because their screen time is precious to them. They are well aware that it is a source of contention in their relationship with you. So after you have had some time to think things through and cultivate a plan, set a time to meet with your children and discuss the changes you'd like to make. When you meet with your children, set a date for when new screen-time policies will go into effect. This gives your children time to adjust to the new policies and have clarity around when they will be enforced.

## Six Screen-Time Strategies

Now that we have unpacked some tips about setting screen-time rules, I want to suggest some screen-time policies that could work well for you and your children. I would love to be able to say that one hour of screen time a day is the perfect plan for every child, but the truth is that every child is different and every family is different. Children have varying needs, interests, and struggles. Every family has unique needs, schedules, and rhythms. Additionally, the current research on screen time indicates that younger children should get less than older kids. For this reason, I do not believe there is one overarching screen-time strategy that all families should employ for the betterment of their children and the harmony of their families. So here are six potential strategies for navigating screen time with your kids in hopes that one of them will work for you or at least spark some ideas for navigating video games with your kids. Don't feel like you have to get your screen-time rules right on the first try, and consider involving your children in the discussion and implementation of these rules.

*Scheduled Screen Time.* For families with set schedules and routines, scheduling a window each day or on certain days that your children can have screen time can work really well. This also teaches your children to schedule their time. If screen time is from 3:30 to 4:30 every day, then they must take on the responsibility of using their screen time during that time frame. They will also be challenged to prioritize what they want to do in ways that can be healthy. For instance, if a neighborhood friend comes by and asks your kid to play outside, they will have a decision to make and might just choose to have less screen time in order to play with a friend.

This strategy might not work for families whose schedules are more sporadic. It may not bother you for your children to miss their screen-time window because that window was the only time you could go grocery shopping, but it will bother your children. Remember, your goal in imposing rules in your home is to set your children up for success. If things keep coming up in your schedule that keep your children from being able to play video games during their screen-time window, they will begin to feel misled, which may mean you need to consider a different strategy.

*First Things First.* If your children value screen time far more than other activities you'd like them to invest in, you can incorporate a system that requires your children to do more important things first. For example, you could require your children to read for thirty minutes and play outside for an hour before they can start their screen time. However, you'll want to be careful not to go overboard with this. Making your kids do things they don't want to do to earn screen time can make them resent that activity and further idolize screen time. For example, a recent study found that children whose parents implement screen-time punishments end up spending more time on screens than those who don't.[13] This is similar to how food-based punishments can actually have the unintended consequence of causing children to develop unhealthy relationships with food.[14] So, instead of framing screen-time limits as punishment, consider framing these as priorities. For example, there are some activities that most children are never going to enjoy, such as their chores. Requiring your child to complete their chores before they play video games teaches that screen time is a privilege and that their contribution to caring for the home you share comes first.

I can say that we have had some success requiring our eldest daughter to read and play outside before getting screen time. If anything, I believe it has increased her interest in reading, and there have been a few times when she had so much fun playing outside that she decided to forgo screen time altogether. We make a conscious effort not to frame these rules as punishments so as not to encourage our children to idolize screen time. Again, situations vary. If your child is already showing signs of video game addiction, you might want to be careful about policies that encourage them to prioritize game time even further. Every child and every family is different, so find what works for you and what best promotes the health of your child.

*Time Limit.* This is the most straightforward approach that works for many families. Simply decide how much screen time you are comfortable with your children having, and set a timer when they start. As your children get older, you can give them the responsibility of setting their own timer and reward them for honoring that schedule.

Something to be aware of with this strategy is that your children are undoubtedly going to protest that they have not reached a save point or are in the middle of a round of a competitive game when the timer goes off. I actually have some sympathy for this because quitting in the middle of a round or before being able to save diminishes the positive feelings of accomplishment games provide. To illustrate what I mean, imagine how you would feel if someone turned off the TV in the middle of the last quarter of your favorite team's football game or during the last five minutes of your favorite show. Conversely, many children will take advantage of this, and their request to get to a save point turns into an attempt to lengthen their screen time. My encouragement is to try to compromise with them on this point; tell them they have five minutes to finish the round or get to a save point. The key here is to try to honor what makes video games enjoyable for them, while still enforcing your children stay close to the time limit you have agreed upon.

There are going to be days when you give in to your children's pleas for more screen time than average. The occasional gift of an additional half hour is fine. Just be careful you don't set a precedent that has you responding to requests for more screen time every day. Setting overly strict and narrow screen-time limits can have the opposite effect we would hope for on some children. If you can, when your children ask for time to complete a level or get to a save point, consider sitting down with them and watching them play. This gives you a chance to ask questions about the games they play, connect with your children, and hold them accountable.

*Seasonal:* Where we live, February is generally cold and rainy, and July and August can be hot and humid—occasionally so much so that playing outside in the middle of the day can be miserable. We also homeschool our children, so February can be particularly rough for my wife because it gets dark early. Everyone feels so cooped up that it starts getting on everyone's nerves. Remember that screen time is not just for your children. You can and should use screen time for things like self-care and/or getting things done around the house. Knowing that certain times of the year are more stressful and cooped up than others, it can be helpful to allow for a bit more screen time at certain times of the year than others. If you do this, just make sure you follow the guidelines: make your rules clear, collaborative, and written down. If you don't, this strategy will be painful for both you and your children when the season ends. Children tend to do well with reminders and balk at sudden changes to their schedule and agenda. My children get a bit more screen time in the summer, but as the school year draws nearer, we remind them that their screen time is about to be reduced.

*Token System.* If your children receive a weekly allowance for doing chores, you might consider increasing their allowance in exchange for them exercising a bit more self-control. You could give your children a certain number of tokens that they could trade in for thirty minutes of screen time or for fifty cents or so added onto their allowance at the end of the week. This approach avoids the pitfalls of making less screen time feel like a punishment while still incentivizing self-control. If your children will likely spend all their tokens on the first day of the week, however, you may want to consider a different approach.

*No Limits or Just Ask.* Most children need clear limits on their screen time, but some children, believe it or not, do well with almost no limits. (I know that this sounds like a recipe for disaster, but it does work in some homes.) Seriously, if your children have a broad set of interests and rarely ever want to spend multiple hours playing games in one sitting, then you may not need to enforce a strict time limit. Another strategy you may want to explore is a "just ask" policy. If they want to watch a show or play a game, just require that they ask permission first. However, if your kids are really into video games or Netflix, this isn't the strategy for you. You'll quickly grow weary and irritable from the number of times they request screen time each day. Your kids will also become irritable in response to the number of times you disappoint them by saying no.

More likely, however, your children just need clear limits and consistent guidelines. Most children do well with clearly laid out guidelines; few things frustrate kids more than rules being altered at the last minute or being confronted for breaking a rule they did not understand. And remember, the above strategies are not guaranteed solutions. If you implement any of these approaches expecting them to fix your child's gaming problem, you will be disappointed. Your children aren't broken. So don't try fixing them. Love them. Part of loving them is setting boundaries for their protection, but that is only one part of the multifaceted work of parenting. You also need to strive to understand and accept the things about them you might not like as much (like their fascination with video games). So in addition to your screen-time rules, you need a plan for connecting with them around their interest in video games.

## Winning the Video Game Battle

Unfortunately, there is no one-size-fits-all solution to how much your kids should be gaming or even what kinds of games your kids should be allowed to play. So far in this book, we have unpacked what games are and how they can be engaged in ways that honor God. We have also unpacked the greatest pitfalls around video games and how to avoid them. I hope you feel more equipped now than you did before, but you probably still feel like you need some next steps to take as you reimagine how you'll handle video games in your home. In the remainder of this chapter, we will discuss some simple strategies to get a better handle on modern video games and how to navigate them with your children.

### *Play Together*

Playing video games with your children is a great way to bond with them. If you are deeply averse to video games, I would say this tip is even more important for you. Nothing says you love your children quite like making an honest effort to do something they love but you hate. If you do this, you'll need to make a conscious effort not to complain the whole time or make fun of the game you play together, as such actions will communicate the opposite message you want to send. Don't worry if you get beat badly. Just try to have a good attitude, ask lots of questions, express genuine curiosity, and try to learn from your child.

A study published in *The Journal of Adolescent Health* looked at the impact of parents and caregivers playing video games with their adolescent girls, which found that kids playing video games with parents is "associated with decreased levels of internalizing and aggressive behaviors, and heightened prosocial behavior for girls."[15] Additionally, "co-playing video games was also marginally related to parent–child connectedness for girls."[16]

## Games Provide Teaching Moments

Researchers from Arizona State University claimed: "Parents miss a huge opportunity when they walk away from playing video games with their kids. . . . Often parents don't understand that many video games are meant to be shared and can teach young people about science, literacy and problem solving. Gaming with their children also offers parents countless ways to insert their own 'teaching moment.'"[17]

Video games provide us with opportunities to talk to our children about perseverance, problem-solving, teamwork, winning and losing, and much more. If conversations like this sound intimidating, here is a simple example from *Forbes* writer Jordan Shapiro:

> Sometimes my six-year-old and I take turns playing various casual games like *Subway Surfers* or *Angry Birds* on the iPad. We cheer each other on. We compare high scores. My eight-year-old got *Halo: Combat Evolved* for his Windows laptop for

Hanukkah. Sure, it's an older game, but he's young. We all crowded around the PC, making suggestions for where he should go and what he should shoot. Later, the three of us discussed why it was okay to shoot imaginary aliens but not people. We thought about what the aliens might represent in a kid's life: anxiety, frustration, anger, etc. I asked them what, in their own emotional experiences, comes on like a monster—uncontrollable, scary, overwhelming. I helped them to see how we might translate the narrative of the game into a lesson in emotional intelligence.[18]

## *Play Better Games*

In chapter 3, I made the case that what troubles me most about video games is the way many of them reward and encourage compulsive play. The good news is that plenty of games out there eschew these compulsive reward loops and, instead, rely on intrinsic rewards. During the *Fortnite* craze, for instance, my team of writers at Love Thy Nerd compiled a list of "8 Better Games for Kids than *Fortnite*"—many of which would be great games to play with your children.[19] However, that was a few years ago. New games are coming out all the time. My friend Andy Robertson, author of *Taming Gaming*, has compiled dozens of lists of recommended games for children and families based on all kinds of different criteria on his website. This is a great resource for finding games that might be appropriate for your children, both in terms of their content and reward structures.[20]

### *Anticipate Irritability and Moodiness*

One of the most common questions I get from concerned parents is: "Why is my child moody or irritable every time I make her turn off her video games?" While intense and consistent irritability or an insatiable desire to play more could be a symptom of video game addiction, most irritability is actually relatively normal. Most children's reaction to turning off a game before completing a level or getting to a save point is comparable to how competitive children react when their sports team loses a game or when they fail to perform as they had hoped. The more deeply engaged you are in an activity, the more disappointing it is to leave it undone. All human beings experience frustration when they can't finish what they started or don't achieve what they had hoped to in each task or challenge. The high level of engagement required of many video games is both a blessing and a curse. It can be a blessing because they require deep focus, critical thinking, and pattern recognition skills. Video games can also be a curse because the more mentally invested we are, the more likely we are to get agitated when our progress is interrupted or destroyed altogether! If you are aware of this tension, you can reduce conflict and irritability in your home by being a bit more proactive in how you talk about gaming with your children:

- Talk to your children before they play video games. If you help your children anticipate how their time playing video games might be frustrating, they will be better prepared to respond. Strive to help them see that gaming is both challenging and fun. Remind them that they can always try again on another day if they fail or don't achieve what they hope to that day.

- Talk to your children about their experience. All children need help learning to process their experiences and, more important, how to decompress from stressful experiences.
- Talk to them about their accomplishments. Help them lower the stakes of their gameplay by helping them acknowledge their achievements and improvements over and above their failures.
- Have a plan for after gaming. Sometimes kids are grumpy because they are hungry or thirsty. Children are complex. Don't assume grumpiness is a character flaw. Consider having a snack or meal ready for when game time is over. You may also think about having a more physical activity in mind for them when they finish playing a video game.

While these suggestions may sound more involved than you'd prefer, remember that such conversations are designed not only to help your children but to help you as well. When you are engaged and willing to help your children process their experiences and the world around them, they are less likely to be overwhelmed by either.

These kinds of conversations help your children grow to be more resilient and less irritable, leading to a happier, healthier, and more productive home for you both.

## Not All Video Game Time Is the Same

As important as setting limits is for your children, there are certain types of play that are better for them than others. For example, your child playing a game online with a friend who recently moved away is different than playing a single-player game. And your child playing team-based video games with a friend or sibling in the same room is different from playing games with friends online. I realize this tip may seem like it contradicts my previous comment about setting clear and consistent rules and boundaries, but if you communicate clearly about occasional concessions for your children to play games for longer than your typical limits when playing with friends, this can be healthy.

## Don't Ignore Conversations about Video Games

If you are worried that your child is obsessed with video games, there is a good chance you've never encouraged conversation on the subject. Even if your child has a problematic relationship with video games, ignoring or rebuking them when they talk about video games is basically the same as ignoring a young child when she or he tries to show you a drawing or a tower made of building blocks.

When you ignore your children's commentary about video games, you might think you are sending the message that video games are problematic. But trust me, that's not the message your children get. The message they receive is not that you aren't interested in their games but, rather, you aren't interested in them. Their brains are still developing, and they are not yet skilled at differentiating between themselves and their interests. So even if you can't stand video games, make an effort to understand them. Taking an interest in your children's interests demonstrates love.

Liking video games is not a requirement to be a good parent, but loving your child is. This requires trying to turn toward their bids for your attention even when those bids require talking about things you might loathe. This doesn't mean you drop everything to talk to your children every time they speak up. But instead of ignoring or rebuking our children, it's better to speak up about our own personal boundaries. Be honest and willing to discuss their interests later: "I'm sorry, I can't talk about *Pokémon* right now because I'm making dinner. Let's talk about it at the table once everything is ready."

## *Use Parental Controls*

Every major platform your children might use to play video games provides you with parental controls to limit and monitor what kinds of content and game experiences they can and can't have. Admittedly, with technology evolving all the time, it can feel overwhelming to understand best practices. Thankfully, the Entertainment Software Rating Board (ESRB) has put together guides for setting up parental controls on just about every major gaming platform.[21] There are also dozens of articles and videos that can help you understand what parental controls are at your disposal, which will walk you through the step-by-step process of setting them up. For instance, you can not only limit what games your children can play based on their ESRB rating, but you can also keep them from playing online or limit them to only being able to communicate with those on their friends list. Most gaming platforms can even allow you to monitor your children's friends list.

## Check Ratings

The best way to know if a particular game is age appropriate for your children is to start with the ESRB ratings.[22] These ratings are printed on the box of physically purchased games and listed at the bottom of any web page where games are sold digitally. If you are like me, you'll want to know more than just the rating. For a deeper dive into the content of games, I highly recommend the reviews by Common Sense Media.[23] This is not a Christian site, so you will want to know that going in, but the reviews are very detailed in terms of outlining the kind of content a piece of media contains. Additionally, their reviews will offer you a sense of the kinds of messages a particular piece of media contains. The website rates the game based on its content, message, and over-all quality. Common Sense Media also features parent-written reviews, where parents list the age of their children before sharing their thoughts on a game, movie, or show. The goal here is merely to stay informed.

## See for Yourself

One of the best ways to see if a particular game your child wants to play is appropriate for them is to watch someone play the game. This is really easy to do. Today, millions of gamers livestream their gaming online on sites like Twitch, YouTube, and Mixer. There is even an active streaming community on Facebook. If you want to get a sense of what a particular game is like, just search for it on one of these sites and watch a few minutes of gameplay. A quick three- to five-minute look at a game will give you a general idea of what the game is like and whether or not it is appropriate for your children.

### *Let Them Be Bored*

One of the biggest mistakes I have consistently made as a parent is always coming to my children's aid when they complain about being bored. This is a mistake for two reasons. First, it puts me on the hook as their go-to strategist to eliminate boredom. This will lead you to exhaustion and keep them dependent on your ideas for activities. Second, boredom is good for children. Every parent faces the temptation to hand their children a screen or turn on the television to remove boredom. However, pediatrician Michael Rich says that children need a diverse menu of online and offline experiences, including the chance to let their minds wander: "Boredom is the space in which creativity and imagination happen."[24]

In other words, when we come to our children's aid every time they are bored, we deny them an opportunity to be creative and exercise their imaginations. I know it's hard not to give in when your children beg to watch another show or play another video game, but if you let them be bored, you might be surprised by what they dream up.

### Screen-Free Zones

In our family mealtime is sacred. Meals are one of the few times each day when my entire family is gathered in the same place for the same purpose. It's a time for my wife and me to focus on our children and for all of us to check in with one another about the day, so we do our best to keep the dinner table screen-free. We feel similarly about our children's bedrooms; we don't allow them to have a TV or video game console in their rooms. Likewise, my wife and I elected not to have a TV in our bedroom.

### Explore Nondigital Games

Looking back to chapter 2, we discussed that video games are a type of game, and games are a type of invaluable play for the development of children. If you'd like your children to branch out and diversify their interests beyond video games, consider some other types of games you could play together. As I'm writing this, *Among Us* is massively popular. It is essentially a digital social deduction game where players work together to fly a spaceship while also trying to figure out who among them is an imposter (i.e., a double agent working against them). One of the coolest things that has arisen out of this is that my kids and their friends on our block devised a way to transport the rules of this game from the screen into our cul-de-sac. They literally developed their own rules for a playground version of *Among Us* outside with one another. It was amazing! Encourage your children to use their love of gaming to design their own playground games.

Board games are one of the fastest-growing industries in entertainment today, and many of the principles and mechanics your children love in video games are translated to the table in today's most compelling board games. Consider starting a weekly board game night. We have a large and very active contention of board game enthusiasts in the Love Thy Nerd Community, many of whom are parents. One of the things I hear from them often is that you'd be surprised how easy it is to get most children interested in board games. Even older children and teens will embrace family game night. As much as teens may act like they don't want to be around their parents, most teens, when asked, say the opposite. No one is more influential on their children than parents are, and despite what they might say sometimes, our kids really do want to spend time with us. Board games give us the opportunity to put our smartphones away and give our undivided attention to our children.

## Find a Community

The average gamer is thirty-one years old. This means that there are plenty of gamer parents out there who understand video games better than you do. Don't feel like you have to figure out video games on your own. Find people who can walk alongside you, answer questions, and point you to resources that help you better understand the digital world your children inhabit. The Love Thy Nerd Community on Facebook or the Love Thy Nerd server on Discord[25] are great places to start, but there are dozens of other online communities where you can ask questions about gaming, screen time, and parenting to other concerned, like-minded parents such as yourself.

# Games Are Mission

Your goal as a parent is not merely to guide your children toward success and independence. Your goal is to disciple them—to embody what it looks like to follow Jesus and encourage and invite them to do the same. To state the obvious: what makes Christian parenting distinctly Christian is the gospel. Helping our children understand that they are part of something bigger than themselves is what the gospel entails (Matt. 28:18–20). I want to take a moment to clarify the mission Jesus calls us to so that we can help our children understand and embrace that mission. Empowering your children to live missionally isn't as difficult as you might think. Living missionally can even incorporate their interest in video games.

A few years ago, I read Tim Chester's book on the mission called *A Meal with Jesus*. In the opening chapter, Chester seeks to clarify the mission Jesus calls us to by asking the following question: "How would you complete the phrase . . . '[Jesus] came to . . .'?"[1]

You would likely answer that Jesus came to die for our sins and be raised from the dead, to save the world, to preach the gospel, or to establish God's kingdom.

There is a second question that is brought up that has to do with us: What should we do? What about us? What are we, as followers of Jesus, supposed to do with our lives? How would you finish the sentence . . . "We should go . . ."?

You might answer by saying we should go preach the gospel, make disciples, engage the culture, change the world, campaign for change, or spread the good news. If we are to understand our purpose, mission, and calling in this life, we should look at how Jesus understood and framed His own calling and purpose. Here are five ways the Gospels complete the sentence "Jesus came to . . ."[2]

1. seek and save the lost (Luke 19:10).
2. preach (Luke 4:43).
3. serve, not to be served (Matt. 20:28).
4. cast fire on the earth (Luke 12:49).
5. eat and drink (Luke 7:34).

Does that last one surprise you? In the referenced verse, Jesus said, "The Son of Man has come eating and drinking, and you say, 'Look, a glutton and a drunkard, a friend of tax collectors and sinners!'"

When Jesus refers to Himself as "the Son of Man," He is not merely pointing out that He is a human being. It is a title found in Daniel 7 for the Messiah, the promised one of God who would reign over all people for all eternity (Dan. 7:13–14). When Jesus calls

Himself the Son of Man, He is claiming authority and power. He is claiming to be King over everything.

By referring to Himself this way, Jesus is embracing His role as God's anointed Messiah who will reign forever. Jesus is essentially saying, "I am King, and I will reign forever . . . and I came to eat and drink." And apparently, He did this a lot. Enough that He was accused, probably by the religious leaders, of being a glutton and a drunk.

Of all the reasons God Himself, the Messiah, the eternal King, claimed to have come from heaven to earth to dwell among us, the last thing we would expect Him to say is something so simple as to "eat and drink." And yet that is exactly what He says in Luke 7:34.

What is so special about eating and drinking? It's something we all do, even if some of us don't give much thought to it. We might say, of course, that Jesus came eating and drinking only out of necessity; after all, everyone eats and drinks. But I'd like to propose that eating and drinking were central ways Jesus established His kingdom on earth.

The Pharisees and scribes, the religious leaders of Jesus's day, noticed this and pounced on Him for it, saying, "The disciples of John fast often and offer prayers, and so do the disciples of the Pharisees, but yours eat and drink" (Luke 5:33 ESV).

Biblical scholar Robert Karis wrote a book about this very subject in Luke's Gospel called *Eating Your Way through Luke's Gospel*, and he says, "In the gospels Jesus is either going to a meal, at a meal, coming from a meal, or teaching about a meal."[3] Many of His parables either include food or are about food. Think of the greatest parable in the gospels: the parable of the prodigal son—it ends with a feast!

Tim Chester says, "Jesus was a party animal."[4] I would push back on this description to some degree because the term "party animal" normally leads us to think of people who get drunk and fail to control themselves. Jesus did neither of those things. That's not what Chester meant to imply though. His point is simply that eating meals with others was a crucial part of Jesus's ministry that many of us have failed to adequately consider.

Jesus turned water into wine to prolong a dying wedding party. On more than one occasion, He multiplied bread and fish to care for those who came to hear Him teach. He commanded His disciples to remember His death with a meal. He ate with Pharisees, with tax collectors, and with sinners. Every meal was intentional and communicated friendship and welcome.

Eating and drinking were central to His mission. We value meals with friends and family today. But in Jesus's day, sharing meals was a cultural expectation, more than just an opportunity to fill one's stomach. New Testament scholar S. Scott Bartchy said:

> Being welcomed at a table for the purpose of eating food with another person had become a ceremony richly symbolic of friendship, intimacy and unity. Thus betrayal or unfaithfulness toward anyone with whom one had shared the table was viewed as particularly reprehensible. On the other hand, when persons were estranged, a meal invitation opened the way to reconciliation.[5]

Jesus's constant practice of sharing meals with people was deliberate, which tells us much about His mission and methodology. This was how He lived out His mission and embodied life in His kingdom.

If you're wondering what this has to do with your child and video games, don't worry. I'm getting there. Jesus was willing to be mocked and criticized by the religious leaders of His day in order to intentionally hang out with sinners—people in need of the hope, love, and purpose that only He could provide. Jesus's practice of sharing meals with people indicates His desire to draw close to them and the value He placed on shared experiences. While Jesus certainly spread the good news in synagogues, He often chose to proclaim the good news about Himself in the context of a shared meal.

Video games provide similar opportunities to love and serve others and invite them nearer. If we fail to help our children see the missional potential of their interests and activities, we are missing a huge opportunity in some big mission fields, and the world of video games is one of the biggest:

- There are 214 million Americans who play video games regularly.[6]
- Sixty-five percent of American households are home to at least one person who plays video games regularly (at least three hours per week).[7]
- In 2020, video game revenue reached $162 billion worldwide (a growth of 35% over 2019).[8]

- The global esports audience is currently estimated to be around 474 million people.[9]

Each year, more than seventy thousand gamers travel to Seattle to attend the Penny Arcade Expo where they spend four straight days sharing their passion for games, seeing new titles, and listening to developers talk about the process of making games. The event sells out within hours, if not minutes. Now, there are Penny Arcade Expos in Boston, San Antonio, Philadelphia, and Sydney, Australia. Dozens of other similar shows draw tens of thousands of attendees: BlizzCon, QuakeCon, and E3, to name a few. Even broader artistic events like South by Southwest now cover video games.[10] And there are even bigger global gaming trade shows than these, such as Gamescom in Cologne, Germany, boasting more than 350,000 attendees a year.[11]

Games are all around us now. Phones and tablets are the fastest-growing game platforms, with revenue expected to reach $116 billion by the end of 2024.[12] You may even have a game or two that you turn to when you are bored or before you go to bed. It's not just games like *Honor of Kings* and *Clash Royale* that are popular. There are more broadly appealing games like *Project Makeover*, *Candy Crush Saga*, *Among Us*, and *Pokémon Go*.

The Boy Scouts now offer a "Game Design" merit badge. You can find video game exhibits in the Smithsonian's American Art Museum and Seattle's Museum of Modern Art. Today, video games are more prevalent and diverse than ever before.

So, what comes to mind when you think of gamers? When you first picked up this book, you probably thought of gamers as young men that live in their parents' basements and survive on Doritos and Mountain Dew. The reality is quite different:

- Seventy percent of gamers are age eighteen or older.[13]
- The average age of gamers is thirty-one.[14]
- Forty-five percent of gamers in the U.S. are female.[15]
- In 2020 we saw a 60 percent growth in playing games among people forty-five to fifty-four years old.[16]

Marketers love talking about different types of gamers—core gamers, casual gamers, serious gamers, mobile gamers—but the reality is that, if we're honest, we are all gamers, or at least most of us are. It's more likely than not that you fit into one of these categories.

In 2014, an article titled "Unpopular, Overweight, and Socially Inept: Reconsidering the Stereotype of the Gamer," included a survey of forty-five hundred gamers detailing their popularity, attractiveness, idleness, and sociability. Researchers found no noticeable differences between those who play games and those who do not.[17]

Even if you don't play games on a console, a computer, or even your phone, your life has been deeply influenced by video games. Their popularity is seeping into all areas of life, with membership and reward programs at stores being heavily influenced by game design. Progress bars and objective lists are used when filling out your LinkedIn profile or your profile for online classrooms. Even specific video games such as *Portal*, *Civilization*, and *Minecraft* are being used in schools across the world to teach coding, physics, political science, and history.

Gamers no longer lurk on the margins. They are everywhere. They are your neighbors, your dentist, and your child's teacher at school. They are your neighbor's kids and your child's teammates. Gamers are both honor students and at-risk kids. The children playing video games now are future doctors, lawyers, and teachers. Yes, some of them will be unemployed, but many will be innovators, inventors, and world changers.

These many millions of gamers share something in common: their eyes light up when they meet someone who shares their affinity for their favorite video game or video game genre. Most gamers, at least those who play regularly, consider their interest in gaming to be part of their identity.

We can respond to video games in several ways. We can turn up our noses. We can decry them for their violence. We can avoid them out of fear that they will take up too much of our time. Or, to the other extreme, we might mindlessly consume them so much that we forget to shower and eat. We can play them so much that when people criticize our games, we respond with outrage and personal attacks. We start caring more about our precious games than we do about people made in God's image. None of these are the approach Jesus would take, and neither should be the approach of thoughtful parents.

Jesus was accused of being a glutton and a drunk because He was intentional about meeting with sinners, spending time with them, and getting to know them so that He might radically transform them. Looking at the statistics, your children's interest in video games might be a phase they will soon grow out of, but chances are that video games will always be a part of their lives, and even a part of their identity. Just as it is crucial that we help our children navigate this interest responsibly, it is also crucial that we help them unlock the missional potential of this unique and massively popular hobby.

I am not suggesting that you hand your children over to video gaming in a bid to reach people for Jesus. I am, however, suggesting that video games provide a common vernacular around which meaningful community can be built. Games have missional potential, so we just need to learn how to unlock that potential responsibly.

If Jesus's earthly ministry took place now, I believe He would play video games for the purpose of loving His neighbors and building relationships with them. I understand this idea might rub you the wrong way, and listen—Jesus certainly wouldn't do anything that would dishonor God or cause harm to people made in His image. However, as we unpacked in chapter 2, playing video games in moderation can be good for us and deepen our relationships with others. Let's help our children see the good that their interest in gaming could bring. This has been my experience: my interest in video games has opened up some of the most meaningful and profound ministry experiences of my life.

## My Story

A little over a decade ago, I started playing video games again. Don't get me wrong, I have always been a gamer, but I decided that I just didn't have time for games while I was in seminary. I also probably gave in to the pressure of some of my seminary peers and pastor friends who basically saw gaming as something for children, something you grow out of, and something that was a waste of time. On top of the social pressures in seminary, I was also poor and newly married, saving up money to start a family.

But the more I studied the Gospels, the more I saw Jesus entering the worlds of nonbelievers, speaking their language, showing genuine interest in what interests them, and speaking into their world.

Around this same time, a debate had begun between film critic Roger Ebert and game designers about whether video games are art. Tom Bissel wrote *Extra Lives: Why Video Games Matter*, a series of essays and memoirs about how video games can be meaningful. Jane McGonigal wrote *Reality Is Broken: Why Games Make Us Better and How They Can Change the World*, which shows how powerful games are as a form of communication with extensive research about the positive potential of games. She went so far as to claim that games can and will make the world a better place.

Since that time, the independent gaming scene and community have grown exponentially, going from a few hundred developers making games in their parents' basements to thousands of people making millions of dollars. *Rocket League*, *Stardew Valley*, *Five Nights at Freddy's*, and *Minecraft* are just a few examples of indie games made by small teams or even by an individual that have turned into multimillion-dollar properties. Games began taking on more meaningful subject matter: *That Dragon, Cancer* (deals with loss), *This War of Mine* (the cost of war), and *Papers, Please* (refugee crises). Then there are games like *Journey, The Unfinished Swan*, or *The Legend of Zelda: Breath of the Wild*, which present players with breathtakingly beautiful worlds to explore and tame. These are games that tell great stories because they involve players in their captivating and meaningful narratives. These examples break through the stereotype that all video games either celebrate violence or tell frivolous stories.

As video games rapidly diversified, so did the way people wrote about them. Game journalists no longer focused only on whether video games are fun or not. They also focused on the meaning, messages, and values each game contained and wrote about the philosophy, ontology (the study of being/existence), and ethics espoused in the video games they were playing. People began writing about what we can learn about ourselves and the world around us from game mechanics. People started discussing game studies and philosophies of play.

As I saw all of this happening and reflected on Jesus's commitment to eating with tax collectors and sinners, I realized there was good work to be done in the world of video games, and I was determined to figure out a way to engage this space missionally and redemptively. At the time, there were very few Christians writing about video games—except to warn them about the most dangerous ones and encourage players not to waste their lives. So I started writing about video games.

I started writing and editing for a site called Christ and Pop Culture, and soon I was writing video game articles for *Relevant Magazine*, *Christianity Today*, *World Magazine*, and many others. I wanted to help Christians see what I was seeing—that games can be meaningful. I wanted people to see that engaging video games can open up new opportunities for building relationships and living missionally.

It was around this same time that I heard about Gamechurch, a ministry dedicated to bridging the gap between the gospel and the gamer. I heard they passed out "Gamer Bibles" at E3. I ended up interviewing the founder of Gamechurch for an article for Christ and Pop Culture, which led the founder of Gamechurch to ask me to work part-time for their ministry for six years. I managed Gamechurch's website, where I led a team of writers to write about video games from a Christian perspective without writing exclusively to Christians. I wanted Gamechurch to be a respected source for video game criticism and discussion while still being clear on our Christian worldview. The goal was to build relationships with gamers by covering video games uniquely and winsomely. This led me to the wild idea of starting a podcast where we talk to game designers about what makes them tick, including their spiritual beliefs.

I was and continue to be determined to write about games as a Christian, to bring my theological education, passion, and perspective to the world of video games. I want to educate people about the intersection of games and spirituality. My writing about video games led to opportunities to cover the Game Developers Conference in San Francisco for *Paste Magazine* and dozens of other shows for Gamechurch and other outlets. I was also interviewing game designers all over the world about their unique perspectives, work, and beliefs, including video game icons like Ken Levine (creator of *Bioshock* and *Bioshock Infinite*) and Rand Miller (cocreator of *Myst* and *Riven*). In other words, my work in the world of video games was opening up incredibly unique missional opportunities. It allowed me to build relationships with all kinds of people whom I would never otherwise have met.

Almost four years ago, Gamechurch went through some organizational changes that made its future unclear, and I felt it was time for me to part ways with them. However, I was still passionate about loving and serving gamers and pointing them to Jesus, so I began praying about how to continue doing ministry in this space. At this same time, some close friends of mine and former Gamechurch colleagues were praying and dreaming similarly. So, we joined forces to start Love Thy Nerd, a ministry dedicated to being the love of Jesus to nerds and nerd culture. The idea was to expand our reach and look for ways to love, serve, and build relationships with all kinds of geeks and nerds rather than focusing only on gamers. We do this by producing thoughtful content that covers and reflects on the diverse aspects of geek and nerd culture (video games, board games, anime, comics, TV, movies, etc.). We also travel to gaming and nerd conventions all over the country and look for ways to serve geeks and nerds there. We recruit and train missionaries to go to these conventions with us, where they spend time serving in the booths of various game publishers and developers. They help lead game demos for attendees or host game events in the convention hall.

We do these things because many nerds have been made to feel unwelcome or out of place at the churches they have visited or participated in, and we want to tell a different story. Jesus intentionally built relationships with all kinds of people who found themselves on the wrong side of the religious power brokers of His day, and we should too. Instead of praying that such people change their minds and show up to our churches, we feel called to go where gamers and nerds are, to take a genuine interest in them, and strive to build real relationships with them.

We live in a deeply divided culture. Games and nerd culture give us the common ground necessary to build relationships with people who otherwise probably wouldn't want anything to do with us. So one of our goals in all that we do at Love Thy Nerd is to build genuine relationships with geeks and nerds for the purpose of pointing them to Jesus. We are also passionate about helping Christians join us in this mission and learn ways they can build genuine relationships with nerds to engage nerd culture missionally. We even have a yearly conference, Love Thy Nerd Con, where we do just that.

## Embracing Games as Mission

I share all this because I firmly believe that your child's interest in video games uniquely positions them to minister to and love people you are not positioned to reach. I am not suggesting that you blindly hand your children over to games and gaming culture in hopes that they'll do some good there. I am, however, suggesting that with your help, protection, and guidance, their interest in video games could be a platform for ministry and meaningful connection. They need your help. Without your guidance, they are far more likely to be mindlessly subsumed by gaming and nerd culture. This might sound like more work than you are willing to put in, but remind yourself of the ultimate goal of parenting: to love your children well. Nurture their interests. Help them avoid falling prey to the potential pitfalls related to their interests, and—if your child is a follower of Jesus—help them see their interests as an opportunity to love their neighbors and point them to Christ.

To understand what this might look like, consider what you might do if you had a son who was really into a sport like baseball. If this was the case, there are some things you are very likely to do. If you don't care for baseball yourself, you'll try to educate yourself on the sport. You'll ask questions; you'll do some research to understand the rules and modern strategies so you aren't lost when you attend your son's games. You may even offer to play catch with him or take him to a batting cage from time to time. If you can afford it, you might let him try out for the local travel team. You may even get tickets and take him to the ballpark to watch a professional game or two. The more commitment he shows and the more enjoyment he gets out of baseball, the more you'll support his hobby.

As he gets older, you'll have more conversations about his future with baseball. If he is one of the select few with the potential of getting a college scholarship, you'll continue to invest in baseball but also stress that this sport is a means to an end—namely, a college education. Statistically speaking, high school will be the last time your child plays baseball regularly, in which case, you'll encourage him to enjoy his time in the sport while it lasts. You'll still want him to play hard and be a good teammate, but you'll encourage him to focus more on making friends on his team than on trying to make it into Major League Baseball. In other words, if you are a Christ-follower, you'd want your child to see the missional opportunities his interest in baseball provides. He may never play competitive baseball again, but he might play in a local softball league someday or coach his kids, both of which will provide opportunities to build relationships with others, love and serve his community, and continue to enjoy his favorite sport.

This is pretty close to the relationship I would encourage you to develop with your children regarding their interest in video games. Video games are something your children are very likely to be doing for a long time. Now is the time for them to learn to do so responsibly and with the bigger picture in mind. Express genuine interest in their hobby. Play with them as you are able. Encourage them to play responsibly, prioritize what is important, build relationships, and help them know their limits. But don't stop there. Encourage your child to dream about how their interest in video games could be a means to glorify God and love their neighbors. Help them start a game night at your church or your home. If your child is interested in making games, consider investing in programming or graphic design courses. Talk to them about what it looks like to embody the love of Jesus through the way they play games online. You don't have to have all the answers to how your children can point people to Jesus through gaming, but you can help them dream.

This task may sound daunting right now if you are still sore from the last blowup you had around video games, but the actions necessary to love your children well regarding their interest in video games are things you've been doing since the day they were born. No one loves your children as much or better than you do; no one is better equipped to help them flourish and live a life of love and impact, so love thy gamer well.

# Notes

## Chapter 1: So Your Kid Is a Gamer?

1. "2020 Essential Facts about the Video Game Industry," Entertainment Software Association, https://www.theesa.com/esa-research/2020-essential-facts-about-the-video-game-industry/.

2. Tim Challies, "Christian Men and Their Video Games," @Challies, September 26, 2016, https://www.challies.com/articles/christian-men-and-their-video-games/.

3. Drew Dixon, "'Video Games Are Stupid' and Other Sins of Communication," *Christ and Pop Culture*, May 8, 2011, https://christandpopculture.com/driscoll-video-games-are-stupid-and-other-sins-of-communication.

4. Douglas Wilson, "Push Function Quit," *Blog & Mablog*, May 27, 2015, https://dougwils.com/books-and-culture/s7-engaging-the-culture/push-function-quit.html.

5. Peter Leithart, "The World's Most Interesting Man," *Patheos*, May 28, 2015, http://www.patheos.com/blogs/leithart/2015/05/the-most-interesting-man-in-the-world/.

6. "2020 Essential Facts About the Computer and Video Game Industry," Entertainment Software Association, https://www.theesa.com/wp-content/uploads/2020/07/Final-Edited-2020-ESA_Essential_facts.pdf.

7. https://www.theesa.com/resource/2020-essential-facts/

8. Ibid.

9. Jamie Madigan, *Getting Gamers: The Psychology of Video Games and Their Impact on the People Who Play Them* (London: Rowman and Littlefield, 2016), xi–xii.

10. "2020 Essential Facts About the Computer and Video Game Industry," https://www.theesa.com/wp-content/uploads/2020/07/Final-Edited-2020-ESA_Essential_facts.pdf.

11. "Distribution of Video Gamers in the United States from 2006 to 2021, by Gender," Statista, https://www.statista.com/statistics/232383/gender-split-of-us

-computer-and-video-gamers/#:~:text=In%202021%2C%20women%20accounted
%20for,women%20during%20the%20previous%20year.

12. Damon Packwood, "The Era of White Male Games for White Male Gamers Is Ending," October 31, 2018, https://qz.com/1433085/the-era-of-white-male-games-for-white-male-gamers-is-ending/.

13. Love Thy Nerd, lovethynerd.com.

## *Chapter 2: Games Are Good*

1. "How Video Gaming Can Be Beneficial for the Brain," October 30, 2013, Max-Planck-Gesellschaft, https://www.mpg.de/research/video-games-brain.

2. Jane McGonigal, *Reality Is Broken* (New York: Penguin Books, 2011), 3.

3. Stuart Brown, "Play Is More than Just Fun," TED Talk, May 2008, video, www.ted.com/talks/stuart_brown_says_play_is_more_than_fun_it_is_vital.html.

4. Brown, "Play Is More than Just Fun."

5. Johan Huizinga, *Homo Ludens: A Study of the Play-Element in Culture* (Boston: The Beacon Press, 1955), 9.

6. Huizinga, *Homo Ludens*, 10.

7. http://www.health.act.gov.au/healthy-living/kids-play/active-play-everyday/benefits-active-play

8. "The Benefits of Play for Adults," HelpGuide, http://www.helpguide.org/articles/emotional-health/benefits-of-play-for-adults.htm.

9. Mansoor Iqbal, "Twitch Revenue and Usage Statistics," Business of Apps, January 11, 2022, https://www.businessofapps.com/data/twitch-statistics.

10. Jonathan Clauson, "Should You Quit Your Job and Stream Video Games All Day?," Love Thy Nerd, September 24, 2018, https://lovethynerd.com/should-you-quit-your-job-and-stream-video-games-all-day/.

11. Todd Hollingshead, "Study: Collaborative Video Games Could Increase Office Productivity," Phys Org, January 29, 2019, https://phys.org/news/2019-01-collaborative-video-games-office-productivity.html.

12. "The Tin Man of Far Cry 2: Part 7," Click Nothing, November 17, 2018, https://clicknothing.typepad.com/click_nothing/2007/10/ludonarrative-d.html.

13. https://www.challies.com/articles/christian-men-and-their-video-games/

14. Huizinga, *Homo Ludens*.

15. Julie M. Albright, *Left to Their Own Devices: How Digital Natives Are Reshaping the American Dream* (New York: Prometheus Books, 2019).

16. Rebecca Harris, "The Loneliness Epidemic: We're More Connected than Ever—but Are We Feeling More Alone?," Independent, March 30, 2015, http://www.independent.co.uk/life-style/health-and-families/

features/the-loneliness-epidemic-more-connected-than-ever-but-feeling-more-alone-10143206.html.

17. "Jordan Shapiro, "A Surprising New Study on How Video Games Impact Children," *Forbes*, August 27, 2014, https://www.forbes.com/sites/jordanshapiro/2014/08/27/a-surprising-new-study-on-how-video-games-impact-children/#46624be67556.

18. Drew Dixon, "The World Entire," January 17, 2013, www.bitcreature.com/editorials/the-world-entire/.

19. "Beating the Video Game Fixation," April 7, 2010, Relevant, https://relevant-magazine.com/culture/tech/features/25208-beating-the-video-game-fixation.

20. Tessa Berenson, "Why Playing Video Games Can Actually Be Good for Your Health," *Time*, September 26, 2015, http://time.com/4051113/why-playing-video-games-can-actually-be-good-for-your-health/.

21. Rachel Kowert, *A Parent's Guide to Video Games: The Essential Guide to Understanding How Video Games Impact Your Child's Physical, Social, and Psychological Well-Being* (North Charleston, SC: CreateSpace, 2016), 37.

22. Andrew Przybylski, "Electronic Gaming and Psychological Adjustment," *Pediatrics: Official Journal of the American Academy of Pediatrics*, August 4, 2014.

23. Przybylski, "Electronic Gaming and Psychological Adjustment."

24. L. Reinecke, J. Klatt, and N. C. Krämer, "Entertaining Media Use and the Satisfaction of Recovery Needs: Recovery Outcomes Associated with the Use of Interactive and NonInteractive Entertaining Media," *Media Psychol*, 14 (2011): 192–215.

25. D. R. Ewoldsen, C. A. Eno, B. M. Okdie, J. A. Velez, R. E. Guadagno, and J. DeCoster, "Effect of Playing Violent Video Games Cooperatively or Competitively on Subsequent Cooperative Behavior," *Cyberpsychol Behavior Society Network*, 15, no. 5 (2012): 277–80.

26. L. A. Jackson, E. A. Witt, A. I. Games, H. E. Fitzgerald, A. von Eye, and Y. Zhao, "Information Technology Use and Creativity: Findings from the Children and Technology Project, *Comput Human Behavior*, 28 (2012): 370–76.

27. A. K. Przybylski, N. Weinstein, K. Murayama, M. F. Lynch, and R. M. Ryan, "The Ideal Self at Play: The Appeal of Video Games that Let You Be All You Can Be," *Psychol Sci*, 23, no. 1 (2012): 69–76.

28. C. J. Ferguson and C. K. Olson, "Friends, Fun, Frustration and Fantasy: Child Motivations for Video Game Play," *Motion and Emotion*, 37 (2013): 154–64.

## *Chapter 3: Games Are Broken*

1. Eric Levenson, AnneClaire Stapleton, and Darran Simon, "Two Killed in Shooting at Jacksonville Video Game Tournament," CNN, August 27, 2018, https://www.cnn.com/2018/08/26/us/jacksonville-madden-shooting/index.html.

2. Audra D. S. Burch and Patricia Mazzei, "Death Toll Is at 17 and Could Rise in Florida School Shooting," *New York Times*, February 14, 2018, https://www.nytimes.com/2018/02/14/us/parkland-school-shooting.html

3. Greg Toppo, "Do Violent Video Games Make Kids Violent? Trump Thinks They Could," *USA Today*, February 22, 2018, www.usatoday.com/story/news/2018/02/20/after-parkland-video-games-back-critics-crosshairs/356654002/.

4. Erik Kain, "Trump Blames Violent Video Games for School Shootings—Here's Why He's Wrong," February 22, 2018, https://www.forbes.com/sites/erikkain/2018/02/22/trump-blames-violent-video-games-for-school-shootings-heres-why-hes-wrong/?sh=55469bfa67f3.

5. http://time.com/5191198/donald-trump-video-game-representatives-meeting/

6. "Addictive Behaviours: Gaming Disorder," October 22, 2021, World Health Organization, http://www.who.int/features/qa/gaming-disorder/en/.

7. Caitlin Dewey, "The Only Guide to Gamergate You Will Ever Need to Read," *Washington Post*, October 14, 2014, https://www.washingtonpost.com/news/the-intersect/wp/2014/10/14/the-only-guide-to-gamergate-you-will-ever-need-to-read/?utm_term=.23c524aac6c1.

8. Peter Farquhar, "Here's What Defenders of Fortnite Refuse to Accept—and It's Ruining an Industry That's Supposed to Be Fun," Business Insider Australia, September 14, 2018, https://www.businessinsider.com.au/heres-what-defenders-of-fortnite-refuse-to-accept-and-its-ruining-an-industry-thats-supposed-to-be-fun-2018-9.

9. Drew Dixon, "Virtual Violence, Video Game Addiction, and the Kingdom of God," CRI, March 1, 2021, https://www.equip.org/article/virtual-violence-video-game-addiction-and-the-kingdom-of-god/.

10. Kerry Shawgo, "Are You Wrong about Video Game Violence?," Love Thy Nerd, August 14, 2018, https://lovethynerd.com/are-you-wrong-about-video-game-violence/.

11. Mike Snider, "Study Confirms Link between Violent Video Games and Physical Aggression," USA Today, August 8, 2019, *USA Today*, https://www.usatoday.com/story/tech/news/2018/10/01/violent-video-games-tie-physical-aggression-confirmed-study/1486188002/.

12. https://www.health.com/healthday/more-evidence-video-games-may-trigger-aggression-kids

13. Shawgo, "Are You Wrong about Video Game Violence?"

14. Toppo, "Do Violent Video Games Make Kids Violent?"

15. Raul A. Ramos, Christopher J. Ferguson, Kelly Frailing, and Maria Romero-Ramirez, "Comfortably Numb or Just Yet Another Movie? Media Violence Exposure Does Not Reduce Viewer Empathy for Victims of Real Violence among Primarily Hispanic Viewers," APA PsycNet, http://psycnet.apa.org/record/2012-28970-001.

16. Christina Regenbogen, Manfred Herrmann, Thorsten Fehr, "The Neutral Processing of Voluntary Completed, Real and Virtual Violent and Nonviolent Computer Game Scenarios Displaying Predefined Actions in Gamers and Nongamers," National Library of Medicine, October 12, 2009, https://www.ncbi.nlm.nih.gov/pubmed/19823959.

17. Kevin Schut, "Should You Play Violent Video Games?," Love Thy Nerd, October 2, 2018, https://lovethynerd.com/should-you-play-violent-video-games/.

18. Drew Dixon, "When Games Matter: Shadow of the Colossus and the Truth about Violence," Christ and Pop Culture, July 19, 2011, https://christandpopculture.com/when-games-matter-shadow-of-the-colossus-and-the-truth-about-violence/.

19. Drew Dixon, "Spec Ops and Moral Complicity," Think Christian, July 13, 2012, https://thinkchristian.reframemedia.com/spec-ops-and-moral-complicity.

20. Mike Snider, "Study Confirms Link between Violent Video Games and Physical Aggression," USA Today, August 8, 2019, https://www.usatoday.com/story/tech/news/2018/10/01/20violent-video-games-tie-physical-aggression-confirmed-study/1486188002/.

21. Snider, "Study Confirms Link between Violent Video Games and Physical Aggression."

22. Drew Dixon, "The Leaderboard: E3 and the American Art of Violence," Paste, June 26, 2012, https://www.pastemagazine.com/articles/2012/06/the-leaderboard-e3-and-the-american-art-of-violenc.html.

23. "International Classification of Diseases 11th Revision," World Health Organization, https://icd.who.int/en.

24. Andy Przybylski and Amy Orben, "Why It's Too Soon to Classify Gaming Addiction as a Mental Disorder," The Guardian, February 14, 2018, https://www.theguardian.com/science/head-quarters/2018/feb/14/gaming-addiction-as-a-mental-disorder-its-premature-to-pathologise-players,

25. Espen Aarseth, Antohony M. Bean, Huub Boonen, et al., "Scholars' Open Debate Paper on the World Health Organization ICD-11 Gaming Disorder Proposal," AKJournal, https://akademiai.com/doi/abs/10.1556/2006.5.2016.088.

26. Andy Przybylski and Amy Orben, "Gaming Addiction as a Mental Disorder: It's Premature to Pathologise Players," The Conversation, February 13, 2018, http://theconversation.com/gaming-addiction-as-a-mental-disorder-its-premature-to-pathologise-players-89892.

27. "What Percentage of People Who Play Video Games Are Addicted?," Neuroscience News.com, November 5, 2016, https://www.google.com/url?q=https://neurosciencenews.com/video-game-addiction-5437/&sa=D&source=editors&ust=1625581313696000&usg=AOvVaw2gxoGbsI954KegVMK905Os.

28. Douglas Gentile, "Pathological Video-Game Use among Youth Ages 8 to 18," *Psychological Science*, https://www.drdouglas.org/drdpdfs/Gentile_Pathological_VG_Use_2009e.pdf.

29. Angela Chen, "Here's Why Experts Are Skeptical of the 'Gaming Disorder' Diagnosis,"The Verge, June 19, 2018, https://www.theverge.com/2018/6/19/17479318/gaming-disorder-who-psychology-video-games-science.

30. Paige Osburn and Gabrielle Healy, "Is Video Game Addiction a Thing?," 1A, NPR, August 8, 2018, https://the1a.org/shows/2018-08-08/from-fortnite-to-final-fantasy-is-video-game-addiction-a-thing.

31. Lee Price, "Playing Games as Addictive as Heroin," *The Sun*, July 8, 2014, https://www.thesun.co.uk/archives/news/962643/playing-games-as-addictive-as-heroin/.

32. Christopher J. Ferguson and Patrick Markey, "Video Games Aren't Addictive," *New York Times*, April 1, 2017, https://www.nytimes.com/2017/04/01/opinion/sunday/video-games-arent-addictive.html.

33. Ferguson and Markey, "Video Games Aren't Addictive."

34. Chen, "Here's Why Experts Are Skeptical of the 'Gaming Disorder' Diagnosis."

35. Rachel Kowert, *A Parent's Guide to Video Games: The Essential Guide to Understanding How Video Games Impact Your Child's Physical, Social, and Psychological Well-Being* (North Charleston, SC: CreateSpace, 2016), 22.

36. Jordan Shapiro, "A Surprising New Study on How Video Games Impact Children," *Forbes*, August 27, 2014, https://www.forbes.com/sites/jordanshapiro/2014/08/27/a-surprising-new-study-on-how-video-games-impact-children/#5afd375c7556.

37. Andrew K. Przybylski, "Electronic Gaming and Psychosocial Adjustment" *Pediatrics*, September 2014, 134 (3) e716-e722; DOI: https://doi.org/10.1542/peds.2013-4021.

38. Russ Pitts, "SimCity Review: Engineering Addiction," Polygon, March 4, 2013, https://www.polygon.com/2013/3/4/4051444/simcity-review.

39. Pitts, "SimCity Review."

40. Sam Machkovech, "Loot Boxes Too Similar to 'Problem Gambling' to Avoid Regulation, Report Says," ARS Technica, April 2, 2021, https://arstechnica.com/gaming/2021/04/uk-report-recommends-regulating-all-loot-boxes-as-gambling/.

41. Debra Bradley Ruder, "Screen Time and the Brain," Harvard Medical School, June 19, 2019, https://hms.harvard.edu/news/screen-time-brain.

42. Alexandre Mandryka, "Compulsion Loop Is Withdrawal-Driven," Game Whispering, August 10, 2016, http://gamewhispering.com/compulsion-loop-withdrawal-driven/.

43. https://www.businessinsider.com.au/heres-what-defenders-of-fortnite-refuse-to-accept-and-its-ruining-an-industry-thats-supposed-to-be-fun-2018-9?fbclid=IwAR3Z3JdpVkFVXXr3p5XSH-9G5YUYA3U9mbqhqadyoNxsvarDNsuZXAJfelQ

44. Zach Carpenter, "Dear *Fortnite* Mom," Love Thy Nerd, July 30, 2018, https://lovethynerd.com/dear-fortnite-mom/.

45. Not all games with microtransactions employ compulsive reward loops. In 2014, for instance, when Microsoft purchased *Minecraft* from Mojang, the former immediately set up an in-game store from which players could buy outfits, texture packs, and mini games. Microsoft did this while eschewing compulsive reward loops. However, many avid gamers despise the concept of microtransactions, believing game makers should not nickel and dime players for more money. As the best-selling video game of all time, there is no doubt that microtransactions have made Microsoft a lot of money. As a parent, you will want to make sure that your children cannot make in-game purchases without your permission, which is easy to set up on most gaming systems and platforms.

46. Drew Dixon, "8 Better Games for Kids than *Fortnite*," Love Thy Nerd, October 30, 2018, https://lovethynerd.com/8-better-games-for-kids-than-fortnite/.

47. "Family Video Game Database," https://www.taminggaming.com/search.

48. "Family Video Game Database," taminggaming.com.

49. "2020 Essential Facts about the Video Game Industry," Entertainment Software Association, http://www.theesa.com/resource/2020-essential-facts-about-the-video-game-industry/.

50. J. Clement, "Distribution of Video Gamers in the United States from 2006 to 2021, by Gender," Statista, August 20, 2021, https://www.statista.com/statistics/232383/gender-split-of-us-computer-and-video-gamers/.

51. Carolyn Petit, "Grand Theft Auto V Review," Gamespot, November 17, 2014, https://www.gamespot.com/reviews/grand-theft-auto-v-review/1900-6414475/.

52. Petit, "Grand Theft Auto V Review."

53. Kowert, *A Parent's Guide to Video Games*, 53.

54. Kowert, *A Parent's Guide to Video Games*, 53.

55. Susan Villani, "Impact of Media on Children and Adolescents: A 10-Year Review of the Research," *Journal of the American Academy of Child and Adolescent Psychiatry*, 40, no. 4 (2001): 392–401. Also see K. A. Earles, R. Alexander, M. Johnson, J. Liverpool, and M. McGhee, "Media Influences on Children and Adolescents: Violence and Sex," *Journal of the National Medical Association*, 2002;94(9); 797–801.

56. A. Brehem, "Navigating the Feminine in Massively Multiplayer Online Games: Gender in World of Warcraft," *Front Psychology*, 4 (2013): 1–12.

57. Jamie Madigan, *Getting Gamers: The Psychology of Video Games and the People Who Play Them* (New York: Rowman and Littlefield, 2016), 7.

58. "Free to Play? Hate, Harassment, and Positive Social Experiences in Online Games," ADL, https://www.adl.org/free-to-play.

59. Nellie Bowles and Michael H. Keller, "Video Games and Online Chats Are 'Hunting Grounds' for Sexual Predators," *New York Times*, December 7, 2019, https://www.nytimes.com/interactive/2019/12/07/us/video-games-child-sex-abuse.html.

60. Kowert, *A Parent's Guide to Video Games*, 54.

61. Anita Sarkeesian and Carolyn Petit, "More Video Games Featured Women This Year. Will It Last," *Wired*, October 15, 2020, https://www.wired.com/story/women-video-games-representation-e3/.

## *Chapter 4: Games Are Complicated*

1. "What Do Teens around the World Think about . . . ?," Global Youth Culture, https://onehope.net/globalyouthculture/, 30.

2. "The Common Sense Census: Media Use by Tweens and Teens," Common Sense Media, https://www.commonsensemedia.org/research/the-common-sense-census-media-use-by-tweens-and-teens-2019.

3. On the subject of social media, I highly recommend checking out the Netflix documentary film *The Social Dilemma*, which unpacks the often troubling ways social media platforms and online apps track our behavior online in order to manipulate our thinking and purchasing patterns.

4. Debra Bradley Ruder, "Screen Time and the Brain," Harvard Medical School, June 19, 2019, https://hms.harvard.edu/news/screen-time-brain.

5. Stephanie Pappas, "What Do We Really Know about Kids and Screens?," American Psychological Association," April 1, 2020, https://www.apa.org/monitor/2020/04/cover-kids-screens.

6. "How to Make a Family Media Use Plan," Healthy Children.org, https://www.healthychildren.org/English/family-life/Media/Pages/How-to-Make-a-Family-Media-Use-Plan.aspx.

7. Elizabeth Hawkey, "Media Use in Childhood: Evidence-based Recommendation for Caregivers," American Psychological Association, May 2019, https://www.apa.org/pi/families/resources/newsletter/2019/05/media-use-childhood.

8. "New WHO Guidance: Very Limited Daily Screen Time Recommended for Children under 5," American Optometric Association, May 6, 2019, https://www.aoa.org/news/clinical-eye-care/public-health/screen-time-for-children-under-5.

9. Wei Wei Chen and Jessica L. Adler, "Assessment of Screen Exposure in Young Children, 1997 to 2014," *JAMA Pediatrics*, 173, no. 4 (2019), https://jamanetwork.com/journals/jamapediatrics/fullarticle/2725040.

10. "NortonLifeLock Study: Majority of Parents Say Their Kids' Screen Time Has Skyrocketed during the COVID-19 Pandemic," Business Wire, August 31, 2020, https://www.businesswire.com/news/home/20200831005132/en/NortonLifeLock-Study-Majority-of-Parents-Say-Their-Kids-Screen-Time-Has-Skyrocketed-During-the-COVID-19-Pandemic.

11. "How to Lazy Genius Kids' Screen Time," The Lazy Genius Collective, May 17, 2021, https://www.thelazygeniuscollective.com/lazy/kidscreens.

12. Ruder, "Screen Time and the Brain."

13. Brandie Weikle, "These Parenting Moves Make the Difference for Kids' Screen Time," *Toronto Star*, January 14, 2019, https://www.thestar.com/life/2019/01/09/these-parenting-moves-make-the-difference-for-kids-screen-time.html.

14. Lindsey Roberts, Jenna M. Marx, Dara R. Musher-Eizenman, "Using Food as a Reward: An Examination of Parental Reward Practices," National Library of Medicine," January 1, 2018, https://pubmed.ncbi.nlm.nih.gov/28951237/.

15. Sarah M. Coyne, Laura M. Padilla-Walker, Laura Stockdale, and Randal D. Day, "Game On . . . Girls: Associations between Co-playing Video Games and Adolescent Behavioral and Family Outcomes," *Journal of Adolescent Health* 49, no. 2: 160–65, https://blog.valleywisehealth.org/negative-effect-of-screen-time-adults-children/https://www.researchgate.net/publication/51515374_Game_On_Girls_Associations_Between_Co-playing_Video_Games_and_Adolescent_Behavioral_and_Family_Outcomes.

16. Cone, Padilla-Walker, Stockdale, and Day, "Game On . . . Girls."

17. "Move Over, Monopoly: ASU Researchers Find Families Bond over Video Game Play," ASU News, July 9, 2013, https://news.asu.edu/content/move-over-monopoly-asu-researchers-find-families-bond-over-video-game-play.

18. Jordan Shapiro, "Research Says Parents and Kids Should Play Video Games Together," Forbes, December 4, 2013, https://www.forbes.com/sites/jordanshapiro/2013/12/04/research-says-parents-and-kids-should-play-video-games-together/.

19. Dixon, "8 Better Games for Kids Than *Fortnite*," https://lovethynerd.com/8-better-games-for-kids-than-fortnite/.

20. "Curated Lists of Amazing Video Games," Family Video Game Database, https://www.taminggaming.com/lists.

21. "Parental Controls," ESRB, https://www.esrb.org/tools-for-parents/parental-controls/.

22. "Ratings Guide," ESRB, https://www.esrb.org/ratings-guide/.

23. https://www.commonsensemedia.org/

24. Ruder, "Screen Time and the Brain."

25. Discord is a chat application that began as a way to help gamers connect and communicate while playing online. It has since evolved and grown. For more information see Rachel Knight's article, "What Is Discord?" Love Thy Nerd, August 4, 2021, https://lovethynerd.com/what-is-discord/.

## *Chapter 5: Games Are Mission*

1. Tim Chester, *A Meal with Jesus* (Wheaton, IL: Crossway, 2011), 13.

2. Chester, *A Meal with Jesus*, 14.

3. Robert J. Karis, *Eating Your Way through Luke's Gospel* (Collegeville, MN: Liturgical Press, 2006), 14.

4. Chester, *A Meal with Jesus*, 17.

5. S. Scott Bartchy, "Table Fellowship," *Dictionary of Jesus and the Gospels,* ed. Joel B. Green and Scot McKnight (Downers Grove, IL: InterVarsity Press, 1992), 796.

6. "2020 Essential Facts about the Video Game Industry," Entertainment Software Association, https://www.theesa.com/resource/2020-essential-facts/.

7. "2020 Essential Facts about the Video Game Industry," https://www.theesa.com/resource/2020-essential-facts/.

8. Teodora Dobrilova, "How Much Is the Gaming Industry Worth in 2022?," TechJury, February 6, 2022, https://techjury.net/blog/gaming-industry-worth/#gref.

9. Christina Gough, "ESports Audience Size Worldwide from 2019 to 2024," Statista, June 1, 2021, https://www.statista.com/statistics/1109956/global-esports-audience/.

10. Jamie Madigan, *Getting Gamers: The Psychology of Video Games and Their Impact on the People Who Play Them* (Lanham, MD: Rowman & Littlefield, 2016), 99.

11. Peer Schneider, Brendan Graeber, Samuel Claiborn," Gamescom by the Numbers," IGN, August 30, 2021, https://www.ign.com/wikis/gamescom/Attendance_and_Stats.

12. Gough, "ESports Audience Size Worldwide from 2019 to 2024."

13. Victor Yanev, "Video Game Demographics—Who Plays Games in 2022," TechJury, February 6, 2022, https://techjury.net/blog/video-game-demographics/#gref.

14. "2021 Essential Facts about the Video Game Industry," Entertainment Software Association, July 13, 2021, https://www.theesa.com/resource/2021-essential-facts-about-the-video-game-industry/.

15. J. Clement, "Distribution of Video Gamers in the United States from 2006 to 2021, by Gender."

16. Dobrilova, "How Much Is the Gaming Industry Worth in 2022?"

17. Rachel Kowert, Ruth Festl, and Thorsten Quandt, "Unpopular, Overweight, and Socially Inept: Reconsidering the Stereotype of Online Gamers," *Cyberpsychology, Behavior, and Social Networking,* 17, no. 3 (March 4, 2014).